D0844114

Introduction

Never having acquired the international master title, I may well fall between two stools in publishing this collection of my best games. The inexperienced reader may be swayed into commenting, "if you can play games like these you ought to be a master," while the expert is more likely to feel, "these games certainly show you aren't — so why bother us with such bilge?" Both, I feel, would be wrong.

It all depends on what you mean by "master". Lasker, in the German edition (1924) of his book *Commonsense in Chess,* asserts that he has never seen a non-master conduct a whole game consistently and consequentially from beginning to end. I am perfectly sure that this was not even true at the time it was written — could any master have surpassed the consistency of non-master E. Z. Adams in punishing Torre's inaccurate opening play in the famous New Orleans miniature? Or, to jump fifty years to the present collection, I cannot help feeling that at least some games in it (such as the struggle of the three pieces against the Queen in the game against Durao) would pass THIS test of a master.

No, mastery demands more than perfection in one game or the winning of one tournament. FIDE is perfectly correct in denying the title to anybody who has not scored either a convincing result in one outstanding tournament, or an even better performance in several lesser events, besides demanding a certain consistency for the retention of the once-acquired title. The fact that I — and many others — are able to beat the occasional grandmaster, or play an occasional noteworthy game, does not make us masters. Yet we — I as well as those anonymous others — are quite able to play chess that is reasonably good and quite worthy of being preserved.

At the same time the very status of non-master imposes certain limitations on the selection of games. The reader will find no quickies under twenty moves in this book (and only two under twenty-five), though I have certainly won my fair share of sacrificial miniatures. A great champion like Botvinnik can afford to include in his *Selected Games* a rather farcical non-game like his 12-move win over Spielmann (which merely shows how poorly an experienced grandmaster like Spielmann could play on occasion). A non-master cannot do so without appearing ridiculous. Thus most of the games in this collection are "real", i.e. fighting games of chess, including a fair number of hard-fought draws and a few losses.

For the same reason I have abstained from perpetuating any mere brainwave or pretty idea and have not included positions from my games. Any player beyond the baby stage of chess may occasionally find a stunning combination in a given position, but such incidents are hardly worth recording. It is the continuity of the play — and, alas, the frequent lack of logical continuity in it — which makes a game what it is.

Of the opposition represented in this volume, fourteen games are against international title-holders, while another seven or eight are against players who have on occasion done quite well in international competition (such as Benkner, Durao, Horseman, Lee, Palme, Reilly, Spanjaard a.o.) without being fully qualified for the master title. I have tried to abstain from including games against "name players" merely because they are "name players". As a result the majority of the games chosen are against strong local amateurs in the countries where I have spent most of my chess career : South Africa, Ireland and Germany.

In selecting and annotating these games I have met with quite a few surprises. Some earlier favourites proved idols with feet of clay. Some rather superficial annotations had to be entirely recast. In short, I encountered an abundance of "agonizing re-appraisals". The balance sheet, however, was not entirely negative : the relative merits of some games emerged only in the course of these re-assessments. That the present notes and presentation are free of major flaws I may hope but dare not really believe : chess is a difficult game. If it were less difficult it would not be so much fun.

For valuable suggestions, assistance in proofreading, setting up diagrams and other help in the process of production, my thanks are due to Messrs. C. H. O'D. Alexander, L. R. Reitstein and J. J. Walsh — a fitting trio of names symbolizing as they do the international, South African and Irish aspects of my chess career.

W. HEIDENFELD.

Dublin, October, 1970.

Some notes on the appreciation of Chess games

A game of chess, like any creation of the human mind, can be appreciated at many different levels. It will appeal in different ways to different people, and it is sure to mean more to one mind than to another. Temperament, knowledge, understanding, the joy of recognition and the contrary joy of meeting something never seen before — all these play their part in the many forms of appreciation.

Tastes differ — in chess as in all other aesthetic pleasures. Some like the simple, others the complex. But even within these categories there are different kinds (not merely degrees) of simplicity and complexity. Most endgames are simple in the material employed, they can be very complex in the stratagems used to win or draw. Most openings are complex, with many competing principles to be weighed against each other; but it is not the complexity encountered in the accurate analysis of a complicated middle game position. Again, a brilliancy prize may be awarded for the clear-cut simplicity of a game like that between Reti and Bogolyubov (New York 1924) or the breath-taking impenetrability of the game between Maroczy and Tartakower (Teplitz-Schönau 1922).

Where a player short of master strength publishes a volume of his best games, such reflections are not mere platitudes. In addition to gratifying his own vanity — whom does he please? Are his simple games convincing enough to serve as models for others — is his analysis of more complex games re- motely deep enough to do justice to the complexities as they arise? Is he knowledgeable enough to know what went before; is his judgment mature enough to invest his generalized comments with authority? If so, why has he not achieved results that would qualify him for some international title? These are valid questions the reader of a volume like the present one may ask its author.

Of course, the large majority of non-competitive players are relatively easy to satisfy. Whatever strategic misconception or major blunder one side has been guilty of — as long as the other exploits it "brilliantly" (which in this context means by the offer of heavy sacrifices), the game is a sure-fire hit. That the overwhelming majority of Morphy's brilliancies — though naturally by no means all of them— were brought off against mediocre defence (just as the overwhelming majority of brilliancies by the "Blackmar" crowd of today) is of minor importance.

Let me hasten to assert that this approach — like any other — is perfectly justified. "There are nine-and-sixty ways of constructing tribal lays, and every single one of them is right," as Kipling has it. But every single one is not right for everybody. Those who regard Morphy's game in the opera box against two aristocratic nonentities as the epitome of worth-while chess are sure of getting a lot of fun out of their hobby; more perhaps than any other type of player. But I do not share their taste.

Even less do I share the taste of those — very knowledgeable — players who expect every game to contribute something, be it ever so little, to the forward march of opening theory. The forward march of opening theory does not exist — like Daumier's conception of the march of human progress it follows a circular route. Here is Reti, one of the greatest 20th century theoreticians, on the King's Indian Defence (quoted from *Masters of the Chess Board*):

". . . Old Indian . . . is bad and is no longer played, *and the same can be said of the fianchetto of the KB* (my italics. W.H.). Here again we are not speaking of variations — the most certain variations are so often refuted — but of general considerations. With the fianchetto development of the KB, Black is supposed to direct the attack against White's strong point. It is impossible for such an attack to succeed. . . ."

Today, fifty years later, the King's Indian (K-fianchetto) Defence is the most frequently-played against the QP. Reti's basic assumption has been shown to be wrong: the attack against White's Q4 is by no means directed against a strong point, but against a seemingly strong point which has lost much of its strength as a result of the move P—QB4 (it is for this reason that White best refrains from P—QB4 in lines where Black has committed himself to the K-fianchetto too early, by playing 1. . . . , P—KN3; as in the Robatsch Defence. This, too, is a generalized statement and may one day evoke the mirth of posterity.).

If this example sounds too old-fashioned to the modern young men, here is what Gligoric has to say about a certain position of the Sicilian Defence (translated from the book of the Portoroz tournament 1958):

". . . In all openings there are certain critical positions brought about by a series of 'objectively strongest moves'. In other days, however, quite different positions were designated as critical in these same openings, and these, too, were regarded as having been produced by the 'objectively strongest moves'. . . . The particular position has a funny history. At first it gave rise to a controversy whether White could win or would have to be satisfied with a draw. Today the question tends to be who actually has the superior game, White or Black. . . ."

Similar examples could be multiplied. At no period in history has any grandmaster or master (let alone a non-master) been distinguished by a maturity of judgment of such sweep as would enable him to say with authority "this opening is good" or "that opening must be discarded". Where his judgment is based on analysis, he may be right (though more often he will be wrong); where it is based on Reti's "general considerations" it is always coloured by his personal approach and predilections and will turn out to be

8

completely faulty as soon as his whole approach is shown, by a later era, to have been mistaken. Similarly, the pendulum may swing back again, and the restored opening system refuted a second time — by entirely different means.

Thus this collection will offer little to those who (in Brinckmann's words) "try to cash in on the cunningly subtle difference between variations A I 6 and C II 7 (a) and, while firing blanks from toy pistols are under the impression they are discharging heavy artillery" (Tournament book of Carlsbad 1929, apropos the game Rubinstein-Johner).

But even after discarding the over-simplified and the over-subtle approach to chess, we are left with an enormous range of differences in appreciation. One such difference is caused by the temperament of the viewer. Let two players of supposedly equal judgment, knowledge and qualifications view a given position in which, say, White has acquired a certain advantage of initiative — he may stand ready to launch the highly promising minority attack on the queen side in generally favourable circumstances. Now the first viewer may well say: "What I like most in this type of game is to follow step by step, how White increases his advantage and wins the game thereby. This really is the highest type of chess." "Not so," says his opposite number. "What I like most in these positions is to see how Black, by imaginative creation of counter-chances, foils White's small theoretical advantage. This is really creative chess."

(For a game that carries this very situation into reality, see the wonderful draw between Marshall and Alekhine at the tournament of New York 1924.) Thus of two equally qualified viewers one may be enraptured by the typical, the other by the atypical in a game of chess, and each will judge the game in accordance with his predilections.

The level and volume of chess knowledge of the viewer is another important factor in the appreciation of chess games. In the present collection the long ending against Patterson may well seem extraordinarily boring to many of those who have the patience to play it over; but to those who know the literature of this type of ending it may be of absorbing interest. Similar differences of opinion are encountered in the assessment (for entertainment value!) of many other endings. Sometimes lack of knowledge prevents even a master from appreciating his own handiwork! In a stroll through the literature of the game I found a really striking illustration of this failure of perception:

In his interesting autobiographical game collection *Chess Secrets*, Edward Lasker publishes many of his games from the great international tournament of New York 1924, regardless of whether he won, drew or lost them; he also includes critical positions from some of these games. Of the first half of the double-round tournament he only omits his games against Capablanca and Marshall. The former indeed contains nothing of interest, but the omission of the latter game (spotty though it is) can only be due to lack of knowledge, as it contains a passage that, viewed in a certain context, is almost unique in the vast literature of the game:

Black: Marshall, to move.

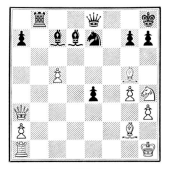

White: Ed. Lasker.

This was the position after White's 27th move. Marshall saw that any move of his N would threaten 28. ..., Q—K4 (threatening mate as well as attacking R and B), and his unfortunate choice was the "elegant" 27. ..., N—B4? As Alekhine remarks in the tournament book, White could well have resigned after 27. ..., N—Q4! (a remark that is perfectly correct even though he misses the most difficult defence, 28. R—K1!, Q—K4; 29. N—B3!, when 29. ..., Q—N6 fails to 30. B—R4, and 29. ..., R—N8 to 30. NxQ, RxRch; 31. B—B1, but the move is refuted by 29. ..., PxN!; 30. RxQ, PxBch; 31. KxP, BxR).

After Marshall's faulty move Lasker found the defence, 28. B—B4!!, and after 28. ..., BxB; 29. NxN, BxN; 30. PxB, B—B2; 31. Q—K3!, Q—K4; 32. Q—N1! with excellent drawing chances, which he spoilt many moves later.

What then is so remarkable about this defence that on the one hand it failed to leave any impression in the mind of the player who found it, and, on the other, moves me to call this one of the most unusual manoeuvres ever seen in an actual game? The wording alone gives the show away: what Lasker executed with the move 28. B—B4 is one of the very rare *anti-Turtons* ever seen in play, though it is a well-known combination in problem composition. It consists in forcing the attacker who wishes to double two pieces of the same gait in such a way as to have the stronger piece in front and the weaker behind (called the *Turton* in the jargon of problemists) into playing the weaker piece across the so-called "critical square" (here Black's K4) and thus into reversing the planned line-up. What is particularly pleasing about this example of a perfect anti-Turton is that, once the obstacle is removed, the B passes back via the critical square and the originally-intended Turton is executed — but the time gained has enabled the defender to stop the mate.

10

Now it is absolutely impossible for even the most modest chess master who *knows* of these contexts and has the good fortune to bring off such a rare combination, not to crow over it and dismiss the game, as Lasker does, with the words: "Marshall made a complicated combination which permitted me to equalize, when he could have won within a few moves. I lost the game through a blunder in the seventh hour of play. . . ." Thus, though Edward Lasker included a chapter on problems in his work *Chess for Fun and Chess for Blood*, his knowledge of this field is clearly deficient — otherwise he would have hailed his game against Marshall as an extraordinary "find" — just as I am doing now. Without a record of this game the literature of chess would be distinctly poorer.

In this context I may quote a very pertinent observation of C. H. O'D. Alexander's in *Chess Treasury of the Air*, where he remarks that on balance his favourite games are those with a touch of queerness about them — where one reaches unusual or original positions. This is indeed one of the greatest sources of pleasure on the chess board. The freakishness can take many forms: the transplant of a problem theme to a game, as in the Lasker-Marshall game; or the material constellation (in the game Euwe vs. Conde, Bournemouth 1939, White played a considerable part of the game with two Rooks and eight(!) pawns against Rook, two Bishops, Knight and three pawns, probably the queerest constellation on record); or the complete or partial blockade of a superior force; or a winning plan introduced by strange retreats (such as N—R1) or equally strange advances (such as N—R8); or under-promotion of a pawn where the normal promotion would fail, and so on and so forth. Naturally this source of enjoyment also comprises all sorts of "records", of which I wish to claim one for myself in the following position from a game Heidenfeld-Littleton, Dublin 1964:

Black: Littleton.

White: Heidenfeld, to move.

Black had sacrificed a pawn to get the R to the 7th with its accumulation of assailable white men. There was indeed a rich harvest, but for both sides, for the next moves were: 20. P—Q3, NxBP; 21. PxN, NxP; 22. RxP, RxR;

11

sequence of 13 successive captures, which I believe is unique in tournament chess. If I have not included this extraordinary game in, this collection it is solely because it was not fully played out and a "lazy" draw agreed a little later in a position with a great deal of interesting play left — the cardinal sin in chess. (The "planned" grandmaster draw is really a lesser sin, for the aim of the master is to win the tournament, not every individual game. As the old Lasker said to the young Botvinnik when the latter could not understand why he had failed to win a certain game at the Moscow tournament of 1935: "Why, young man, do you have to win every game?" But an unforced draw of convenience in a position rich in play is a different matter: it is a wasted opportunity, not merely a disappointment to the onlooker.)

Before concluding this formless ramble through the aesthetics of chess, I may state my personal view: what most captures *my* imagination and arouses *my* admiration is neither the perfect technique nor the stunning combinative power of one partner, but the clash of personalities of both. The "Battle in the Balance" in which both sides try to calculate the virtually incalculable, and risk everything to gain everything (such as the games assembled in my little volume *Grosse Remispartien*) has always held a particular fascination for me. It may be a Quixotic attitude, but the analysis of positions that *defy* analysis has always seemed a rewarding task to me — I only wish I were better at it. Of course, what seems incalculable to me, may not be incalculable to a grandmaster; but the frequent analytical errors that permeate not only the games, but even the books, of the most famous masters, do not suggest that this easy way out is as readily accessible as one may be inclined to think. Thus, summing up, let me say that I find most worthy of appreciation everything that shows how difficult chess is — not how easy it can be made to look. And it is very largely, though not exclusively, from this point of view that the present collection has been compiled.

Game No. 1.

It is not by accident that the most "brilliant" game — in the conventional meaning of the term — should be the first in this collection. Most brilliant games, adorned by heavy sacrifices of material, occur when the opponent has treated the opening too badly to counter the pressure you bring to bear on his position. (Of course there are much deeper and far more elaborate real brilliancies, but their number is small and, with very few exceptions, they bear the brand of the very greatest masters.)

Now, when you are young you are usually far more aggressive over the chessboard than in later years; and also — unless you live in the USSR or some similar chess battery establishment — your opposition will not be out of the top drawer. Provided you are endowed with a reasonable amount of imagination, THAT is the time for conventional brilliancies, such as the following game played in the Berlin league matches 1929.

Black: K. Zietemann.
Giuoco Piano.

1. P—K4	P—K4
2. N—KB3	N—QB3
3. B—B4	B—B4
4. O—O	N—B3
5. P—Q4	B x P

Black refuses to go into the Max Lange Attack with 5. ..., PxP; 6. P—K5, P—Q4. Like many gambits it leads to the rapid opening of lines and early complications — to whose advantage is still doubtful after many decades of practical tests.

6. N x B	N x N
7. P—B4	N—B3?

An old mistake. The player who has accepted the gambit pawn must often sacrifice position for crude development; that is part of the price he has to pay for his pawn. Naturally Black would, if the opportunity presents itself, like to free his game in one go by advancing the QP two squares, but he can't have everything. Correct is the developing move 7. ..., P—Q3; 8. PxP, PxP; 9. B—N5, when White has a little pressure for his pawn but hardly enough to equalize.

8. B x P ch!	K—B1

Or 8. ..., KxB; 9. PxP, NxP; 10. Q—R5ch, N—N3; 11. P—K5.

9. P x P	QN x P
10. B—N3	P—Q3
11. B—N5	B—N5?

This looks like a developing move with the gain of a tempo, but the white Queen moves away with a strong threat (13. BxN, PxB; 14. Q—R6ch). Black should have aimed at neutralizing the white Bishop by some sequence such as 11. ..., Q—K2; 12. N—B3, P—B3; to be followed by 13. ..., B—K3.

12. Q—Q2	K—K2
13. Q—B4	R—KB1
14. P—KR3!	

It is now clear that Black has lost, not gained, time with his Bishop. He cannot play 14. ..., B—K3; 15. BxB, KxB; 16. Q—B5ch, and 17. QxP (for the Knight will be pinned wherever the King has gone on move 16).

14. ...,	B—Q2
15. N—B3	P—B3

If 15. ..., B—B3 (so as to give the King a flight-square), the weakness on K3 is again fatal: 16. Q—B5, threatening both 17. Q—K6 mate and 17. QxP.

16. QR—Q1!	

Asking Black to break the bind by 16. ..., P—KR3.

16. ...,	P—KR3
17. R x P!	

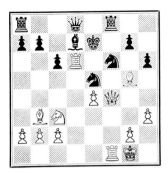

I still remember the excitement that gripped me as I made this move. After I had decided on it, I jumped up and went round the room to calm down and then go once again over the eventualities of the combination before finally committing myself.

17. ...,   Q—N3 ch(?)

This merely hastens the end. If Black accepts the Rook at once, there would have followed 17. ..., KxR; 18. QxN(K5)ch!, KxQ; 19. B—B4ch, K—Q5; 20. R—Q1ch, K—B4; 21. B—K3ch, K—N5; 22. R—Q4ch, K—B4; 23. R—Q5 dbl. ch., K—N5; 24. P—R3 mate. This King hunt was frequently seen in 19th century games, but what distinguishes the combination is the possibility of a defence demanding a second Queen sacrifice that drives the King to the other end of the board: 17. ..., N—N3!; 18. RxN!, NxQ; 19. R—K6 dbl. ch., K—

B2; 20. RxNch, K—N1; 21. RxRP dis. ch., R—B2; 22. BxRch, K—B1; 23. R—R8 mate.

Black's best defence was 17. ..., N—N3!; 18. RxN!, and now 18. ..., Q—N3ch. White must then not continue as above, with 19. K—R1?, NxQ; 20. R—K6 dbl. ch. because in the position after RxRP dis. ch. Black would have the resource QxB; PxQ, PxR; and White discovers that he has sacrificed too much material. White would therefore continue with 19. Q—B2!, PxR; 20. QxQ, PxQ; 21. BxP, followed by 22. B—N7, winning three pawns for the exchange with the much superior game. As so often happens against the best defence (Anderssen's Immortal Game against Kieseritzky is the classic example), even the stormiest combinations may lead only to a small material or positional advantage, and the early mate is due entirely to the defender's lapses.

18. K—R1   K x R

Now 18. ..., N—N3; is no longer playable: 19. BxNch, RxB; 20. RxB ch!, KxR; 21. Q—N4ch, K—K2 (otherwise the black N is lost after RxR); 22. RxR, KxR; 23. Q—K6ch, K—N4; 24. Q—B5ch, K—R5; 25. Q—N4 mate.

19. Q x N(K5) ch   K x Q
20. B—B4 ch   K—Q5
21. R—Q1 ch   K—B4
22. B—Q6 mate.

Game No. 2.

Meeting one's first "real" international master is a milestone in the life of every aspiring youngster. Here was I, in a game of the Berlin league 1930, facing a man who had won several international tournaments and beaten Capablanca and Bogolyubov, Niemzovich and Reti. Determined to make it hard for my opponent, I chose a little-known gambit line involving a piece sacrifice, which goes back to the great Hungarian master, Breyer; and I chose it without knowing it properly. Looking back over the game today I wonder whether I would make such determined — and unconcerned — use of my counter-chances now as I did at the time.

White: F. Sämisch.

French Defence.

1. P—K4   P—K3

I have played all sorts of things against 1. P—Q4, but have remained faithful to the French Defence against the KP.

2. P—Q4   P—Q4
3. N—QB3   N—KB3
4. B—N5   B—K2
5. P—K5   KN—Q2
6. P—KR4   P—QB4
7. N—N5

Today 7. BxB is usually played first and only on 7. ..., QxB instead of the recommended 7. ..., KxB) does White play N—N5. The reader will find this line in game No. 18, against A. R. B. Thomas.

7. ...,   PxP

And here modern theory recommends 7. ..., P—B3; as in the famous miniature, Rossetto - Stahlberg, Vino del Mar 1947.

8. N—Q6 ch   K—B1
9. Q—R5   NxP

The wrong way of giving up the piece. The Breyer line continues 9. ..., P—KN3; 10. Q—R6ch, K—N1; 11. BxB, QxB; 12. NxB, Q—N5ch; 13. K—Q1, N—QB3! when Black has plenty of play for the material he has shed.

10. BxB ch

Of course not 10. NxB?, BxB; 11. QxB, P—B3!

10. ...,   QxB
11. QxN   N—B3
12. Q—N3   P—K4
13. Q—QR3

Protecting the N and stopping the possibility, Q—N5ch, if the Knight has to move. But now came a surprise for Sämisch, who afterwards complained, in his inimitable style, to one of his team mates: "Here the master found a very strong move".

13. ...,   P—QR4!
14. NxB

Black threatened 14. ..., N—N5; and this looks the best way out. If, e.g. 14. Q—B5, N—N5!; 15. O—O—O White slithers into a lost game after 15. ..., B—B4; 16. NxP, QxQ; 17. NxQ, R—B1.

14. ...,   RxN!

Black's compensation for the piece consists not so much in the two pawns (which, in fact, he jettisons a little later), as in his impressive lead in development (especially of the King!). It would therefore be wrong to open the N-file for White by 14. ..., QxQ — let the other fellow do the exchanging.

15. QxQ ch   KxQ
16. K—Q2   R—B2
17. R—R3   P—K5
18. R—QN3   KR—QB1
19. N—K2

After the great massacre White has developed purposefully. Black can utilise his central pawn cluster and command of the QB-file only if he gets his N into play. The N is tied to the defence of the QP? — Well, there is a perfectly good King available to take over!

19. ...,   K—Q3
20. R—N5   K—K4!

Regardless!

21. P—B4   N—K2
22. P—QN3

Now Black could save his pawn by P—R5. But this is not good enough: White threatens to play P—N3, N—B4 and B—R3, when Black's proud centre will be assaulted by all white pieces. The Rook on N5 must be dislodged no matter at what cost.

22. ...,   R—B4
23. RxNP   N—B4
24. RxP(?)

At the cost of his two extra pawns Black has kept his centre intact. White might have done better to refuse the second pawn and return the R to N5. If then 24. ..., PxP; 25. PxP, N—Q3;

15

26. RxR, RxR; 27. N—Bl! (not the tempting 27. P—B4ch, PxP e.p.; 28. PxP, NxPch; 29. K—K1, P—Q6; 30. N—N3, N—N7; with a strong bind). Now Black either has to allow White's dead Bishop to be exchanged or he cannot get the QBP, since 27. ..., P—Q6; can be answered with 28. **BxP!**

However, Sämisch, by this time left with 16 moves to make in 1½ minutes, cannot do full justice to the position and plays the natural move.

24. ...,	P x P
25. P x P	P—Q6

Of course not 25. ..., RxP?; 26. RxNch, **etc.**

26. R x N ch

In extreme time pressure, White returns his extra material to free his game. If now 26. ..., KxN; 27. N—N3ch, K—B5! (not 27. ..., K—K4?; 28. R—K1, attacking both centre pawns); 28. NxP, KxN; 29. BxPch, K—Q5; 30. R—K1, R—K4; the black centre is liquidated and White retains two pawns for the exchange. In the circumstances I felt justified in proposing a draw, which was immediately accepted.

The question arises whether White could have achieved more without the sacrifice. Obviously the Knight must move:

(a) 26. N—Bl? (so as to punish 26. ..., RxP? with 27. NxPch,

PxN; 28. BxP, R—B5; 29. R—K1ch), N—Q3!; 27. RxP, NxP ch; 28. K—K1, P—Q7ch; 29. K—K2, P—Q8(Q)ch!; 30. Kx Q, N—N7ch; 31. K—K1, RxN ch; 32. RxR, RxRch; 33. K—K2, N—Q6! and wins.

(b) 26. N—N3?, NxN; 27. PxN, RxP; 28. RxP, R—B7ch; 29. K—K3, P—Q7; 30. R—Q1, R(1)—B6ch; 31. K—K2, P—K6; 32. R—K7ch, K—Q5; and both sides have to repeat moves. Nor does, in this line, 28. BxP, R—Q1! give White any hope.

(c) 26. N—B3! (best). Now Black must not play 26. ..., N—Q3; 27. R—K7ch!, when 27. ..., K—Q5; can be answered with 28. BxP!, PxB; 29. R—Q7! or 27. ..., K—B3; with 28. Rx KP or 27. ..., K—B4; with 28. P—N4ch!, giving White splendid chances in all variations. Best would be the modest 26. ..., RxP; 27. R—B1, R—N5; 28. NxP, RxR; 29. KxR, KxN; 30. BxPch, KxB; 31. RxN, P—R5; when White remains a pawn to the good but the black King's position seems to be sufficient compensation.

Undoubtedly a fascinating introduction to "big" chess!

Game No. 3.

Young players usually see the be-all and end-all of chess in sacrifices (the same, incidentally, applies to some that are not so young. I well remember how, the first time I ever took part in a simultaneous display — against Bogolyubov — a white-haired old geezer went round the room, asking solicitously at every board: "Has the master sacrificed yet?"). The beauties of positional chess are not usually appreciated till much later. Thus, in the following game, Black offers what is really a sacrifice "on spec.", which is (I think wrongly) declined. Having got away with it, Black acquires the superior position and then sacrifices for gain, which netted him the prize for the most brilliant game of the tournament. This game was played in the South African championship at Johannesburg, 1935.

White: Dr. M. Blieden.

Budapest Counter Gambit.

1.	P—Q4	N—KB3
2.	P—QB4	P—K4
3.	P x P	N—N5

I have never cared for the Fajarowitz line, 3. ..., N—K5. The Budapest is not really meant to be an "attacking" line, but an attempt to exploit pawn weaknesses created by White's early pawn moves (including P—QB4). Black therefore should aim at recovering his pawn without incurring pawn weaknesses of his own.

4.	P—K4	N x KP
5.	N—QB3	

The usual follow-up in this, the sharpest of all lines in the Budapest, is 5. P—B4, followed by 6. B—K3.

5.	...,	B—B4
6.	P—B4	KN—B3
7.	N—B3	P—Q3
8.	P—KR3	

So as to stop B—KN5 which, pinning the N, would increase Black's hold on the black centre squares. Having induced the opponent to this loss of time, Black should simply castle and aim at an early P—KB4. Instead he dares White to go into hair-raising complications.

8.	...,	N—R3?!
9.	P—R3	Q—B3!
10.	B—K2?	

White hopes to complete his development without further untoward incidents, but in this he is deceived. Should he have called Black's "bluff" by 10. N—Q5, Q—N3; 11. P—QN4?

Dr. Blieden was a most intrepid defender of any material his opponents might throw his way. He was of full master strength with a tremendous capacity for taking pains. Kostic, the globe-trotting grandmaster of the twenties, called him the strongest player south of the Equator. Lest it be thought that this was merely the usual blarney Kostic used to dish out everywhere to endear himself to his varying audiences, I may mention that in this case he committed himself black on white in the pages of the *Wiener Schachzeitung*.

Thus, Dr. Blieden's declining a challenge of this sort suggests that he was not at his best on this occasion (as was proved by his further loss to Driman in the following round). After 10. N—Q5!, Q—N3; 11. P—QN4!, Black's best is 11. ..., QxPch; 12. Q—K2, and now either (a) 12. ..., QxQch; 13. BxQ, N—Q5; 14. PxB, N—B7ch; 15. K—B2, NxR; 16. B—N2, P—QB3!; 17. BxP, PxN; 18. BxR, N—B7. White stands somewhat better, though the position is unclear; or (b) 12. ..., BxPch; 13. PxB, QxQ ch; 14. BxQ, N(B3)xP — and though Black has three pawns for the piece, I doubt whether they are full compensation.

The line 11. ..., Q—N6ch; 12. K—Q2, O—O; recommended in *My Book of Fun and Games* is inadequate after 13. PxB, NxP; 14. Q—K1!, for if then 14. ..., N—N6ch; 15. K—B3, QxQch; 16. NxQ, NxR; Black can save neither his N nor his QBP and remains with a mere Rook for two minor pieces.

10.	...,	N—Q5
11.	R—B1	O—O
12.	N—Q5	N x N ch
13.	B x N	

If 13. RxN, Q—R5ch; forces the K to Q2, since 14. K—B1 loses the exchange to 14. ..., B—KN5!

13.	...,	Q—R5 ch
14.	K—K2	P—QB3

17

15. N—B3   B—K3

White has been completely outplayed. All black pieces are on excellent squares and all that is required is the rapid opening of further lines against the white King.

16. P—QN3   KR—K1
17. K—Q3   P—Q4!

Here it comes. If now 18. BPxP, PxP; 19. PxP, B—B4ch; 20. B—K4, RxB; 21. NxR, R—K1; 22. R—K1, B—B7; and wins; if in this line 19. NxP, QR—B1; holding the white King in his uncomfortable position and threatening 20. ..., BxN; 21. PxB, Q—B3. If 18. KPxP, B—B4ch; etc. Thus White tries to flee with his King.

18. BP x P   P x P
19. K—B2   P x P
20. B x P   QR—Q1
21. Q—K1   Q—B3
22. B—N2   B—Q5
23. P—B5

White has no choice as both 23. ..., N—B4; and 23. ..., B—KB4; was threatened. But now the force Black has accumulated against the white King explodes.

See diagram opposite.

23. ...,   B x P ch!
24. K x B   N—B4 ch
25. K—B2

Position after White's 23rd move.

Or 25. K—R2, Q—QN3; 26. R—QN1, Q—N6ch; 27. K—R1, RxB!; 28. NxR, QxP mate — a pretty variation given by Brian Harley in the *Observer*.

25. ...,   Q—QN3
26. R—QN1

Parrying the threat of RxB — at the expense of the Queen.

26. ...,   Q—N6 ch
27. K—B1   N—Q6 ch
28. B x N   R x Q ch
29. R x R   B x N
30. B—B2

Or 30. R—Q1, BxBch; 31. RxB, Q—B6ch; 32. R—B2, Q—R8ch; 33. K—Q2, RxBch!

30. ...,   B—Q7 ch
Resigns.

Game No. 4.

Despite its shortcomings, the following game — played in the Johannesburg championship 1936 — has remained one of my favourites. The opening, Leonhardt's variation of the Caro-Kann, has now been a foible of mine for close on 35 years (see also the games against Pachman and Dr. Lange, Nos. 26 and 28), and it is only relatively recently that the line has had theoretical recognition from the "high-ups". And the final combination, I still believe, has the charm of a composed problem.

Black: K. Dreyer.
Caro-Kann Defence.

1. P—K4   P—QB3
2. P—Q4   P—Q4
3. P—K5   B—B4
4. N—K2   P—K3

5. N—N3   B—N3
6. P—KR4

This line was first played by the great connoisseur of opening play, Paul Saladin Leonhardt, in his game against Preusse at the tournament of

Magdeburg 1927. For many years I was the only player to follow in his footsteps. In view of the following note, the reason for this neglect is difficult to understand.

6. ...,   P—KR3

Always played in the few games that have featured this line. Yet Boleslavsky, in his recent book on the Caro-Kann, regards 6. ..., P—KR4; as the only positionally acceptable reply. Why, will be explained in the next note.

7. P—R5   B—R2
8. B—Q3

In later years I preceded this move with 8. P—QB3, so as to avoid the line 8. ..., BxB; 9. QxB, Q—R4ch; 10. P—B3, Q—R3; but Boleslavsky maintains that White has no reason to fear the exchange of Queens. He quotes a game Aruntjunoff-Chalibeili, Azerbeidjan 1960, which continued with 11. QxQ!, NxQ; 12. P—KB4, P—QB4; 13. P—B5, PxQP; 14. PxKP, PxKP; 15. PxP, B—N5ch; 16. K—K2, N—K2; 17. P—R3, B—R4; 18. R—KB1, R—QB1; 19. K—Q3, with a substantial spatial advantage. The cramping power of the KRP is an important factor in the ending.

8. ...,   B x B
9. Q x B   P—QB4
10. P—QB3   N—QB3

Now 10. ..., PxP; 11. PxP, Q—R4ch; 12. N—B3, Q—R3; can be answered with 13. N—N5! (Heidenfeld-Dunkelblum, Amsterdam 1962). But the text is not the most accurate — Black should combine pressure against Q5 and QN7 by first playing Q—N3, so as to stop the development of the QB (compare game No. 28).

11. B—K3   Q—N3
12. N—Q2   P x P

12. ..., QxP; 13. R—QN1, P—B5; 14. RxQ, PxQ; is obviously bad for Black.

13. B x P   B—B4
14. B x B

This and the following moves are unlikely to be the best available — why not, e.g., 14. N—N3? As the game goes, Black should have had no difficulty in getting a very satisfactory position.

14. ...,   Q x B
15. N—N3   Q—N3
16. P—KB4   KN—K2
17. R—QN1   R—QB1
18. N—K2   N—B4?

But this — with the advance of the KNP in the offing — is asking for trouble. As Miss Menchik has pointed out in *Chess,* Black should have played 18. ..., O—O; e.g. 19. N(N3)—Q4, NxN; 20. NxN, P—B3!; 21. O—O, PxP; 22. PxP, N—B3. The whole idea of the build-up with P—K5 and P—KR5 is to make it hard for Black to get the move P—KB3 in; and thus to make the most of the control of the black squares. Here Black has the chance for P—KB3 and does not take it.

19. P—N4!   Q—K6
20. R—Q1!

Turning the tables: Black has defended the Knight by attacking the Queen; White simply defends the Queen and thus attacks the Knight. The net result is that the passive white Rook goes from QN1 to Q3, while the black Knight has to return to the departure point.

20. ...,   Q x Q
21. R x Q   KN—K2
22. N(K2)—Q4   P—KN4

Desperately looking for counterplay. Simple and good now was 23. PxP e.p., and any master would have played it, but White prefers a more colourful line of play "for kicks".

23. N—N5   K—B1
24. N—Q6   R—B2
25. N—N5   R—B1
26. N—Q6

Both partners were short of time, so a little repetition is a welcome relief.

26. ...,   R—B2
27. O—O!

Better late than never! It is this pawn sacrifice White had in mind when making his 23rd move.

27. ...,   P x P
28. R x BP   N x P
29. R—K3   N(K2)—B3
30. N—QB5   K—K2?

This move allows a most surprising decision. It was asserted at the time that 30. ..., R—K2; would have forced White to take the draw by repetition of moves (31. N—B8, 32. N—Q6, etc.), but White has the promising continuation 31. P—N4! If then 31. ..., P—N3; 32. NxKPch!, RxN; 33. NxBP, NxN; 34. RxR, N any and Black is badly tied up and must lose at least one more pawn. Or 31. ..., R—N1; 32. P—N5!, RxPch; 33.

RxR, NxR; 34. PxN!, PxP (forced); 35. R—B3, and now either 35. ..., K—N2; 36. R—N3, P—B4; 37. N—B8! or 35. ..., N—K4; 36. R—B4, with the threat of R—QR4 to be followed by N—B8, freeing the QRP. This cannot be prevented by 36. ..., N—Q2; because of 37. NxPch!, RxN; 38. RxPch. In all these lines White has clearly considerable winning chances — though none as clear as after the move in the text.

31. N x BP!

This leads to a neat echo play in one variation and the fourfold setting of one geometrical motif in the other.

31. ...,   R—KB1

If 31. ..., NxN; 32. NxKP!, and now (a) 32. ..., R—Q2; 33. N—B5 dis. ch., N(B2)—K4; 34. N—Q3, K—K3; 35. NxN, NxN; 36. R—B5, etc., or (b) 32. ..., R(2)—B1; 33. N—N5 dis. ch., N(B2)—K4; 34. N—B3 as above .

32. N x N   R x R

If 32. ..., NxN; 33. RxR, KxR; 34. NxKPch, forking the other Rook.

33. N—N6 ch   K—Q3
34. N x R   P—K4

34. ..., KxN; would allow fork No. 3.

35. N(B4)—Q3   R—N2
36. R—N3   P—K5
37. N—B4!

For on KN2 the Rook is still within reach of the demoniac Knight!

Resigns.

Game No. 5.

Played in the South African Championship at Cape Town 1947, the following game provides an object lesson in the exploitation of the "Wyvill Formation", a term coined by Kmoch for the double pawn complex P—Q4, P—QB3, P—QB4. Though Wyvill, known from the London tournament 1851, may have been the first to exploit this complex, the subject was not systematically discussed till the late Aron Niemzovich made a special study of it in the twenties of this century (refer particularly to his famous game against P. Johner, Dresden 1926). The formation crops up frequently in the Niemzo-Indian

Defence, especially in the lines in which Black omits to play P—Q4. Since the days of Niemzovich, who unreservedly condemned the double pawn, our judgment, largely as a result of Botvinnik's games, has become more lenient, but in certain circumstances — such as obtain in the present game — the Wyvill pawn complex is still fatal.

White: A. O. Lewinberg.

Dutch Defence.

1. P—Q4	P—KB4
2. P—QB4	N—KB3
3. N—QB3	P—K3
4. P—KN3	B—N5
5. P—QR3?	

To waste a move so as to bring about the "Wyvill" in a position like the present is certainly bad. Here the position is fundamentally different from, e.g., the Sämisch variation of the Niemzo-Indian: the KBP, already on the fourth rank, stops the formation of a strong white centre by P—KB3 and P—K4. An eventual P—K4 can now be answered with either PxKP or even P—B5 and Black, not White, will obtain attacking chances on the King side, in addition to his sounder formation on the other wing.

5. ...,	B x N ch
6. P x B	P—Q3
7. B—KN2	O—O
8. N—R3	Q—K2
9. O—O	QN—Q2
10. P—B3	P—K4
11. P—K4	N—N3
12. Q—Q3	B—K3!

"P—Q5 is, almost without exception, a serious error if it incurs the freeing of square QB5 for a black piece . . ." (Kmoch, *Die Kunst der Bauernführung*). In the present position White is forced to commit this error (Black having abstained from blocking the position by an early P—QB4). From now on White conducts a hopeless fight against the occupation of his QB5 by a black Knight.

13. P—Q5	P x P
14. P x P	B—Q2
15. N—B2	Q—K1

Now. with the Queen side paralysed, Black re-groups for the "normal" King-side attack in the Dutch Defence. This attack is hard to meet exactly BECAUSE an exchange of many pieces will leave White helpless on the Queen side.

16. B—K3   N—R5!

With the threefold positional threat of a direct attack against QB6, an indirect attack (via QN7) against QB5, and occupation of his QB4. A Knight on the edge is not always weak.

17. KR—K1   Q—R4
18. R—R2

If White's previous move had any meaning, it could only have been to remove the KR from attack in case of the pawn sacrifice P—B5, B—N4; P—B4, N—N7! Perhaps White should have tried to get some air by this sacrifice rather than being slowly strangled. With the text he plays his R into a focal position on QB2 where it can be used to stop both NxP and N—N7, but the Rook blocks squares the white Queen needs.

18. ...,   P—QN3
19. R—B2   N—N5
20. N x N   B x N
21. B—KB1?

21

Freeing the square QB5 for the black Knight — for one move! But that move is enough. However, the white position was already extremely difficult. If, e.g. 21. R—KB2, RxR; 22. BxR, N—N7; 23. Q—B1, N—Q8! wins material. Or if 21. R—KB1, RxR; 22. BxR, R—KB1; 23. R—KB2 (not 23. B—K2?, BxB; 24. RxB, NxP!), RxR; 24. BxR, B—Q8!; 25. K—N2 (to stop 25. ..., Q—B6; 26. B—K1, QxQ; 27. BxQ, N—N7; and 28. ..., B—N6), N—N7; 26. Q—K3, B—N6; 27. Q—B3, Q—N3; wins material. If in this line 26. Q—Q2?, B—B6ch!; 27. K—N1, BxP; 28. QxN, Q—B6; mates or wins the Queen. In all these lines the weakness of White's Queen side stops him from (otherwise welcome) exchanges.

21. ...,	**R—B6!**
22. B—K2	**N—B4!**

Magnis itineribus, as Julius Caesar used to write, the Knight careers across the board to destroy the white King position by a sacrifice.

23. Q—Q2	**N x P**
24. Q—B1	**N x NP!**
25. B x R	

The Knight is inviolate — but so is the Rook!

25. ...,	**B x B**
26. Q—N2	**R—KB1**
27. B—B2	**N—K5**
28. B—N3	**N x B**
29. P x N	**Q—R8 ch**
30. K—B2	**B—N5 dis. ch.**
Resigns.	

Game No. 6.

Up to the time of the present game K. F. Kirby used to be my hoodoo; in fact, I had lost four tournament games to him without as much as scoring half a point. This game, played in the South African championship at Durban 1949, has remained my only win, all our subsequent encounters ending in draws. Even my opponent will agree, however, that none of the other games reached the standard of this battle and that I am not taking "unfair advantage" of the one game I managed to win.

Black: K. F. Kirby.

French Defence.

1. P—K4	**P—K3**
2. Q—K2	

In those days Kirby was the opening expert *par excellence* in South Africa, and one couldn't get out of the books fast enough against him. This harmless eccentricity of Chigorin's gives me a meaty, full-bodied game just to my liking.

2. ...,	**N—K2**
3. P—KN3	**P—Q4**
4. P—Q3	**P—KN3**
5. B—N2	**B—N2**
6. P—KB4	**P—N3**
7. N—KB3	**B—N2**
8. O—O	**O—O**

9. QN—Q2	**N—Q2**
10. P—B3	**N—QB4**
11. R—Q1	**Q—B1?**

So far the opponents have merely sniffed at each other. Here I expected 11. ..., B—QR3; complementing Black's previous move in trying to force a clarification in the centre. I had, however, decided to "unclarify" the position still further by answering 11. ..., B—QR3; with 12. N—K1?! With the text Black leaves the KN unguarded and thus allows an unfavourable simplification.

12. P x P!	**N x P(Q4)**
13. N—K4	**N—Q2**
14. P—Q4	**B—QR3**

"Too late," she cried. White has

22

now obtained a very promising formation with a King-side attack by P—KN4—B5 in the offing. Black must therefore challenge the white centre, but the advance of the QBP allows White the majority of pawns on the Queen side and his pieces are just as well posted for an exploitation of this feature. In other words, White has clearly won the opening.

15. Q—KB2	P—QB4
16. P x P	N x P(B4)
17. N—K5!	

| 17. ..., | N x N |

Black cannot play 17. ..., BxN?; 18. PxB, N—Q6; 19, Q—Q4, Q—B5; 20. N—B6ch, K—R1 (or 20. ..., K—N2; 21. RxN!, QxR; 22. B—R6 ch!, K—R1!; 23. QxQ, BxQ; 24. NxN, PxN; 25. BxR, RxB; 26. BxP); 21. NxN, PxN; 22. B—B1!, QxQch; 23. PxQ, N—N5 (or 23. ..., NxB; 24. BxB and Black loses a piece); 24. B—Q2!, winning the exchange, since 24. ..., N—Q6; is answered with 25. B—R6. This is more convincing than the line given in the S.A. Chess Year Book 1950, which after 19. ..., Q—B5; continued with the immediate 20. B—B1?, QxQch; 21. PxQ, NxB?; 22. BxB, N—N5; 23. B—N7, QR—N1; 24. N—B6ch, K—N2; 25. B—B3, with the double threat of N—Q7 and RxN, for Black could play 21. ..., N(6)—N5! instead of NxB.

| 18. B x N | B—N2 |

19. B—N2	Q—B2
20. P—B4	—B3
21. Q—K2	

Stopping 21. ..., N—K5.

21. ...,	KR—Q1
22. B—K3	B x B
23. Q x B	R x R ch
24. R x R	R—Q1
25. R x R ch	Q x R
26. Q—QB2!	

White has achieved his object. The black pieces cannot enter the game at any point and the white majority is ready to advance.

26. ...,	B—B1
27. P—QR3	B—B4
28. K—B2	N—K5 ch

Here Kirby offered the draw, under the impression that White would have to accept the sacrifice: 29. QxN?, Q—Q7ch; 30. K—B3, Q—Q8ch; etc.

| 29. K—B3! | P—B4? |

Disconcerted by his miscalculation, Black commits the decisive error. Until now the ending was merely unfavourable for Black—with the square K4 no longer under his control it is lost. It is instructive to see how the command of his K5 square assists White in the exploitation of his Queen-side chances.

30. P—QN4	B x B
31. K x B	Q—Q3
32. Q—Q3	Q—B2
33. Q—Q7	Q x Q
34. N x Q	K—B2
35. P—B5	

One step nearer to the passed pawn, the ultimate object of any pawn majority. Black cannot answer 35. ..., K—K2; 36. PxP, KxN; 37. PxP.

| 35. ..., | P x P |
| 36. N x P | N—Q3! |

It is easy to see that 36. ..., NxN?; leads to a hopeless pawn ending. And there is no time for counter-threats on the other side by 36. ..., N—B3; because White can simply ignore them: 37. K—Q3, N—N5; 38. K—B4,

NxP; 39. K—N5, N—B8; 40. K—R6, NxP; 41. KxP, P—R4; 42. P—N5, P—R5; 43. P—N6, P—R6; 44. P—N7, P—R7; 45. P—N8(Q), P—R8(Q); 46. Q—B7ch, K—N1; 47. NxP!, Q—R2; 48. K—N8, and wins, would be a plausible line. Black therefore has to defend passively and hope for the best.

37. P—QR4   P—KN4!

A valiant attempt to keep the white King out. But why pick up stray pawns on the King side if the game is to be decided on the other wing?

38. K—Q4	**P x P**
39. P x P	**K—K2**
40. N—Q3	**N—K5**
41. N—K5	**K—Q3**
42. N—B4 ch	**K—K2**
43. P—N5	**N—B3**
44. P—R5	**N—Q4**
45. P—N6	**P x P**
46. N x P	

Of course not 46. P—R6?, N—N5;

47. P—R7, N—B3ch.

46. ...,	**N—B2**
47. K—B5	**N—R3 ch**
48. K—N5	**N—B2 ch**
49. K—B6	**N—R3**
50. N—B4	**K—Q1**
51. K—N6	**N—B2**
52. P—R6	**K—Q2**
53. P—R7	**Resigns**

for if 53. ..., N—R1ch; 54. K—N7, N—B2; 55. N—K5ch! (of course not 55. P—R8(Q)?, NxQ; 56. KxN, K—B3; etc.) and Black lands in a complete *zugzwang*. If 55. ..., K—Q3; 56. K—N8, N—R3ch; 57. K—B8, N—B2; 58. K—N7 wins. If 55. ..., K—Q1; 56. P—R4!, P—R4; 57. P—R8(Q)!, for with the square KN6 available to the white Knight, the black King can safely be allowed access to Q4—K5.

This and the game against Wolpert (see game No. 20) I consider my two best achievements against South African players.

Game No. 7.

The third game of my match against the New Zealand, later British champion, R. G. Wade, played in 1951 at Paignton, must surely rank as one of the wildest ever to have developed from the very quiet opening line adopted. Both attack and defence (or rather counter-attack) are conducted with a kind of ferocious brilliance that illuminates the fact that chess is not so much art or science as struggle.

Black: R. G. Wade.
Old Indian Defence.

1. P—Q4	**N—KB3**
2. P—QB4	**P—Q3**
3. N—QB3	**P—K4**
4. P—K3	

A very quiet line with which White retains all options (it occurred, e.g., in the Boleslavsky-Bronstein match 1950). After 4. PxP, PxP; 5. QxQch, KxQ; White would not have the slightest advantage (compare the entirely different situation in the note after the 4th move in the game against Bennett, game No. 14).

4. ...,	**P—B3**
5. N—B3	**QN—Q2**
6. B—K2	**B—K2**
7. O—O	**O—O**
8. Q—B2	**R—K1**
9. P—QN3	**Q—R4**

This move has good authority, having been adopted by several Russian masters, but its merit as against the immediate Q—B2 escapes me.

10. B—N2	**N—B1**

11. P—QR3	B—N5
12. P—QN4	Q—B2
13. QR—B1	

At first glance it looks as though this Rook ought to be kept for one of the files further West and that the KR should go to the QB-file. Actually White's threat of a general advance on the Q-side is a mere feint at this stage, with the idea of forcing the opponent's pieces into passive positions and then striking on the other wing.

13. ...,	QR—Q1

White's advantage in space prevents Black from finding a move which would be equally effective against any of the various methods of ending the tension in the centre, and would therefore not ultimately turn out to be a waste of time. This is a problem often confronting the defender in a cramped position.

14. P—Q5!	P x P
15. P x P	R—B1
16. P—R3	

Now Black has to make up his mind. If the B remains on the K-side (B—R4), White would commence Queen-side operations in earnest. In answer to the expected reply in the text the scene changes completely.

16. ...,	B—Q2
17. B—Q3	P—KN3
18. N—Q2	N—R4
19. P—N4	N—N2
20. P—B4	P—KR4

Offering a piece so as to take over the attack himself. The alternative, 20. ..., P—B4; would have been answered with 21. Q—Q1.

21. P—B5	B—KN4
22. P—B6	B x P ch
23. K—N2	P x P
24. P x N	K x P

Of course not 24. ..., PxPch?; because 25. K—B3 would win a second piece.

25. P x P	B x P!

First things first: square KB3 must

be taken from the white Rook. Thus, if e.g. 25. ..., Q—Q1; at once, 26. R—B3!, BxN; 27. QxB, BxP; 28. R—N3; or if 26. ..., B—B5; 27. RxB!, PxR; 28. N(B3)—K4 dis ch, K—N1; 29. N—B6ch, QxN; 30. BxQ, RxQ; 31. RxR, etc.; if 26. ..., Q—N4; 27. N(Q2)—K4, QxPch; 28. R—N3.

26. B—N5!

Clearing square Q3 for the Queen with the gain of a move, even though the attacked Rook cannot be taken immediately.

26. ...,	Q—K2
27. Q—Q3	B x N

With the Queen safely anchored at Q3, Black cannot afford to give up further material (the KR) to keep the black Bishop on the board.

28. Q x B	N—Q2
29. N—K4	

29. ...,	B—R6 ch!

This ingenious sacrifice is the culmination of Black's play. In the postmortem Wade doubted its wisdom, but he is really committed by now. If e.g. 29. ..., R—KR1; 30. RxR, RxR; 31. R—KR1, B—R4; 32. B—K2, R—KR1; 33. BxB, RxB; 34. RxR, PxR; 35. B—B1. Or if 29. ..., P—B4; 30. R—KR1!, B—R4 (if here 30. ..., PxN; 31. Q—R6ch, K—B2; 32. Q—R7ch, K—B3; 33. Q—R4ch, K—B4; 34. RxR gains a lot more material); 31. BxN, QxB; 32. Q—N5 wins. After the text White has to play very accurately.

30.	K x B	R—R1 ch
31.	K—N2	Q—R5
32.	Q—B4!	

Only this forceful move breaks the black attack. It protects the Knight, stops the check on R7 and prepares to deal with the check on R6 as in the text. The seemingly strong 32. BxN?, on which Wade had counted, would have allowed 32. ..., QxNch; 33. R—B3, QR—Q1!!; after which the B could neither remain on the KR3—QB8 diagonal nor be protected (34. R—B7?, RxB!). A possible continuation might have been 34. R—K1, R—R7ch!; 35. KxR, QxR(B6); 36. B—R3, R—KR1; 37. Q—N2, RxBch; 38. QxR, Q—B7ch; followed by QxR. With the reduced material Black's three pawns would be full value for the piece.

32.	...,	Q—R6 ch
33.	K—B2	R x R
34.	R x R	R—R5

Black has nothing better. The sug-gestion of the British Chess Magazine, 34. ..., P—B3; is obviously an over-sight because of 35. BxN.

35.	Q x BP ch!	K x Q
36.	N—N5 ch	K—B3
37.	N x Q	R x N
38.	R—B1	R—QN6
39.	K—N2 dis ch	K—N2

If 39. ..., K—K2; 40. B—B1. The rest is simple.

40.	B x N	R x B ch
41.	R—B2	R—N6
42.	R—B3	R—N7 ch
43.	K—N3	K—R3
44.	R—B6	K—N4
45.	R x P	R—N6 ch
46.	K—B2	R x RP
47.	B—K8	K—B5
48.	R—B6 ch	K—K5
49.	P—Q6	R—R7 ch
50.	K—N3	K—K6
51.	R—B3 ch	Resigns

for if 51. ..., K—Q5; 52. P—Q7; if 51. ..., K—K5; 52. BxPch: and if 51. ..., K—K7; 52. R—B2ch.

Game No. 8.

The final game of the same contest, which Wade had to win to draw the match and I had to draw to win the match. Few of the last-round battles I have been engaged in over the years have equalled the strain and intensity of this game. Both of us threw everything we had into the battle and were completely exhausted at the end.

White: R. G. Wade.

Queen's Gambit Declined
(Lasker Defence.)

1.	P—Q4	N—KB3
2.	N—KB3	P—Q4
3.	P—B4	P—K3
4.	B—N5	B—K2
5.	P—K3	P—KR3
6.	B—R4	O—O
7.	N—B3	N—K5
8.	B x B	Q x B
9.	Q—B2	QN—B3?

Very much a "non-masterly" move, both tactically and positionally. White could safely accept the pawn: 10. PxP, NxN; 11. QPxN, N—Q4; 12. PxP (not, as Wade suggests in *Chess*, 12. B—K2 because of 12. ..., N—N5; followed by NxBP when White does not have much), but he is so worried about losing the initiative in this important game that he hardly notices how little Black would get for his pawn.

| 10. | P—QR3 | N x N |
| 11. | Q x N | N—N1! |

A decision harder to make than many a Queen sacrifice, Months before my trip to Europe I had made up my mind never to uphold faulty decisions. The Knight does not co-operate with the rest of the black forces; so instead of trying to justify its placement on QB3 I rather lose two tempi.

12. R—QB1   P—QB3
13. B—Q3?

Played with a view to an attack that ultimately fails. Much better was the routine 13. N—K5, to be followed by P—B4 as soon as the black Knight — belatedly — appears on Q2. This would have been the proper punishment for Black's earlier sins.

13. ...,   N—Q2
14. B—N1   P x P
15. Q—B2   P—KN3
16. Q x BP   P—K4!

Into the teeth of the gale.

17. B x P!

The expected reply, over which Wade took one hour and ten minutes — the longest time ever taken against me over one move by anybody. If instead 17. PxP, NxP; 18. NxN, QxN; 19. BxP?, QxNP; 20. O—O, B—K3; 21. Q—K4, B—Q4; with advantage to Black.

17. ...,   P—K5!

It appears that Wade wasted a lot of time over the possible reply, 17. ..., N—N3; which he has discussed at length in *Chess*. Black, however, never considered that move: the sim-

ple reply, 18. Q—B5!, would have left White with a clear advantage. In fact, I played the text almost at once.

18. N—K5   N x N
19. P x N   B—K3

Determined to fight it out with the extra piece. 19. ..., QxKP; 20. Bx KP, QxNP; 21. O—O, would have given White a promising initiative.

20. Q x KP   P x B
21. Q x P ch   K—R1
22. Q x P ch   K—N1
23. Q—N6 ch   K—R1
24. Q—R6 ch

Making up some of his leeway on the clock.

24. ...,   K—N1
25. P—K4

Threatening to get his Rooks into the attack.

25. ...,   R—B2
26. R—B3   R—N2
27. P—B4

As Wade points out, 27. R—N3 would be answered with 27. ..., B—B5; preventing White's castling and thus the active deployment of his KR. Nor has he the time to prevent this by 28. P—QN3, because after 28. ..., B—N5; the white pawns would begin to fall. It is this potential for active counter-play which induced Black to opt for the line adopted on move 16.

27. ...,   R—KB1
28. R—N3   R(1)—B2

Having weathered the attack as well as avoided simplification to an ending in which the white pawn phalanx would be irresistible, Black now gets his counter-play.

29. R x R ch   R x R
30. O—O   Q—B4 ch!
31. K—R1   Q—B5
32. R—Q1

After Wade's subsequent recommendation, 32. R—KN1, B—N5!; the winning chances would be with Black.

32. ...,   B—Q2
33. P—K6!   B x P!

A surprising rejoinder, which allows the Rook to infiltrate. If, however, 33. ..., QxP(K5)?; 34. QxRch!, KxQ: 35. PxB wins immediately; and if 33. ..., QxP(K3); 34. QxQch, BxQ: White, with his four passed pawns and the Rook on an open file, would have a fine ending.

34. R—Q8 ch

Here again Wade considered for a long time before submitting to the forced perpetual check that results from this move. If 34. P—B5, B—Q2; 35. P—B6, R—B2; the black King seems perfectly safe.

34. ,..,   K—B2

35. Q—R5 ch

and drawn by perpetual check.

This is the type of game that lives in one's memory as a "real game of chess". Normally games published in biographical game collections make the protagonist appear as a sort of Superman rather than struggling for equality, and on the whole the present collection is no exception. Yet I hope to have included an adequate number of games (compare e.g. Nos. 30 and 42) to show how to get out of a self-created mess and thus to correct the entirely erroneous image created by those smooth wins.

Game No. 9.

The two games I played as top-board against Canada's Dr. Bohatyrchuk — erstwhile over-the-board champion of Soviet Russia, with a score of $3\frac{1}{2}$-$\frac{1}{2}$ against Botvinnik! — in the correspondence match between Canada and South Africa (1950/52) have taught me a healthy respect for the demands this form of chess makes on its adherents. The work I had to invest in these two games ($+1$ -1) probably exceeds that required by all the other 49 games in this book put together. Except for some "games" to test the merits of a disputed position, I have been faithful to the vow I made on that occasion: Never again!

Black: Dr. F. Bohatyrchuk.

Two Knights' Defence
(Ulvestad variation).

1. P—K4	P—K4
2. N—KB3	N—QB3
3. B—B4	N—B3
4. N—N5	P—Q4
5. P x P	P—N4?!
6. B—B1	Q x P
7. N—QB3	Q—B4
8. B x P	B—K2
9. P—Q3	

Here White had to decide on his long-range plan of campaign. He is threatened with further loss of time unless he makes the white centre squares safe for his pieces, and he is also in danger of having to surrender, sooner or later, his pair of Bishops.

He therefore aims at making K4 the pivot of his position, holding it with a pawn which would control both Q5 and KB5, and recalling the B to plug the open Q-file in case of need.

Shock tactics, based on the temporary weakness of Black's QB3 and KB2, would recoil horribly: 9. Q—B3?, B—N2; 10. P—QN4, Q—Q3!; 11. QN—K4, NxN; 12. QxPch, K—Q1; 13. NxN, Q—Q5!; 14. N—B3, R—KB1; 15. Q—Q5ch, QxQ; 16. NxQ, N—Q5; and wins.

9. ...,	O—O
10. KN—K4	N x N
11. P x N	N—Q5
12. B—Q3	B—K3
13. O—O	P—N3

28

On the immediate 13. ..., P—B4; 14. PxP, Black would have to recapture first with the B and then with the R (because of the threat of Q—Q5ch). But after the double exchange White would continue with 16. B—K3, and 17. Q—N4, levelling development and remaining with a sound extra pawn.

14. K—R1!   QR—N1

White's last move was made in expectation of 14. ..., P—B4; to which he could now reply 15. P—KB4! If then the speculative 15. ..., P—N4?!; the answer 16. PxNP, P—B5; would have given Black a certain amount of play for his two pawns. But White had prepared the continuation, 16. PxBP!, BxBP; 17. BxB, RxB; 18. B—K3, NPxP; 19. BxN! If then 19. ..., QxB; 20. Q—N4ch, R—N4; 21. Q—K6ch, K—B1; 22. N—Q5, Q—B4; 23. N—B6 wins immediately, while if 19. ..., PxB; 20. N—K2, regains the extra pawn without danger.

15. P—B4   P x P
16. B x P   B—N4

If 16. ..., B—Q3; 17. P—K5, Bx KP; 18. N—K4, Q—Q4; 19. P—B4, Q—R4; 20. P—QN4, RxP; 21. B—Q2, etc.

17. Q—Q2   B x B
18. Q x B

Not 18. RxB?, RxP; 19. N—R4, Q—N5!

18. ...,	**P—KB3**
19. N—R4	**Q—QR4**
20. P—QN3	**N—B3**
21. Q—K3	**N—K4**
22. QR—Q1	**QR—Q1**
23. Q—B5	**Q x Q**
24. N x Q	**B—N5**
25. R—Q2	**R—Q3**
26. K—N1	**B—B1**
27. R(B1)—Q1	**KR—Q1**
28. P—KR3	**P—KR4**

After the game Dr. Bohatyrchuk claimed that the immediate 28. ...,

K—N2; would have stopped White from playing for the exchange of Rooks because the black King could then enter KB5. So he could indeed.

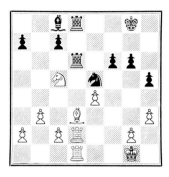

Play might go: 28. ..., K—N2; 29. K—B2, K—R3; 30. K—K3, K—N4; 31. B—R6, RxR; 32. RxR, RxR; 33. KxR, BxB; 34. NxB, K—B5; 35. NxP, K—N6; 36. N—Q5, KxP; 37. NxP, P—R4; 38. K—K3, KxP; 39. K—B4, P—R5!! A surprising sacrifice, which seems to save the game. White would have had to look for a different method of winning.

29. K—B2	**K—R2**
30. K—K3	**K—R3**
31. B—R6	**P—R5**
32. B x B	

If 32. P—B4, Black's best is probably 32. ..., N—B2. If he plays 32. ..., BxB; then not 33. NxB, RxN!; 34. RxR, RxP; 35. R(1)—Q2, R—R6; winning another pawn, but simply 33. RxR.

32. ...,	**R x B**
33. P—B4	**R—B3**
34. R—Q5	**R—K1**
35. K—Q4	**N—B2**
36. R—K1	**R—K4**
37. R—Q7	**N—N4**
38. P—QN4	**R—Q3 ch**

Black is running out of moves and has to exchange Rooks, at the same time denying the white Knight access to his QB5. But a new weakness results: the pawn on Q3. From here to the end White, by simply defending against the transitory black threats, forces the opponent to weaken his position more and more.

39.	R x R	P x R
40.	N—Q3!	N—K3 ch
41.	K—K3	R—KN4
42.	K—B2	K—N2
43.	R—K3	K—B2
44.	N—K1	P—R4
45.	N—B3	R—R4
46.	P—R3	R—R1
47.	R—Q3	P x P
48.	P x P	R—QN1
49.	P—N5	N—B4

50. R—R3

With a protected passed pawn and the open R-file White no longer needs the extra pawn.

50.	...,	P—N4
51.	K—K3	R—K1
52.	K—Q4	P—N5
53.	R—R7 ch	K—N3

After the forced exchanges of the next few moves the position of the black King will safeguard White's remaining K-side pawn owing to the fork on KR4. If, in the final position, 56. ..., P—R6; 57. PxP, R—N6; 58. R—R3, and Black is helpless.

54.	P x P	R x P ch
55.	K—Q5	R x NP
56.	P—N6	Resigns.

Game No. 10.

Played at the Ilford Congress 1953, the following game may, or may not, have enriched the literature of chess. What it almost certainly has done is to enrich the literature of bridge! My opponent, having vacillated between the two games for many years, may well have been induced by the "progressive squeeze" to which he is subjected in this very game, to give up chess completely (I believe Ilford was his last serious tournament) and concentrate on bridge to such an extent that he very soon became one of the leading players and writers, first in England and more recently as the bridge correspondent of the New York Times in the USA.

Black: A. Truscott.
Sicilian Defence.

1.	P—K4	P—QB4
2.	N—KB3	P—Q3
3.	P—Q4	P x P
4.	N x P	N—KB3
5.	N—QB3	P—QR3
6.	P—QR4	P—K4
7.	N—N3	B—K3
8.	B—KN5	QN—Q2
9.	N—Q5	

Although this commits White to capturing on Q5 with a pawn, ending Black's worry — always with him in the K4 variations of the Sicilian — about the weakness of his Q3, this move is not without point. White in-tends to hold the black Q-side in an iron grip, by getting pawns to QR5 and Q5 (the latter protected by the QBP). In a way this is the transference to the Q-side of the build-up with pawns on K5 and KR5 to which I am partial in the Caro-Kann Defence (compare games 4, 26 and 28). The following moves are easy to understand.

9.	...,	B x N
10.	P x B	B—K2
11.	B—K3	R—B1
12.	P—R5	Q—B2
13.	P—QB4	O—O
14.	B—K2	

This position is quoted by Barden,

in his "A Guide to Chess Openings" as a model of a favourable position for White — an assessment based on the potential of the white Q-side majority and the lack of counter-play for Black.

14. ...,   **N—K5**
15. P—B3!

Since the black-squared B is the soul of the Q-side siege, White has to sacrifice this move (see his 18th) to stop B—N4, which would now be answered with 16. B—N6, winning a piece.

15. ...,   **N(K)—B4**
16. N x N   **P x N**

From now on Black has to be on the alert against an eventual P—QN4.

17. O—O   **P—B4**
18. P—B4   **P—K5**

It is understandable that, in view of White's passed pawn and strong Bishops, Black wants to keep the position closed, but in doing so he drifts into complete passivity.

19. Q—Q2   **N—B3**
20. K—R1

So as to provide a hide-out for the B on KN1 in case of need.

20. ...,   **P—KN3**
21. KR—Q1   **KR—Q1?**

Tactically allowing the very push he should have tried to stop. Quite apart from that, what was the objection to giving the village idiot on K2 a useful function by 21. ..., B—Q3?

22. P—QN4!   **R—Q2**
23. QR—B1   **K—N2**

Obviously the pawn was taboo on the previous move. If it is captured at this point, there might follow: 23. ..., PxP; 24. P—B5, QxRP; 25. P—Q6, K—N2 (on the previous move the QP could not be taken because of the pin, and if the black King now remains on the white diagonal, White would continue with 26. R—R1 and 27. Q—R2ch, winning the Bishop); 26. Q—N2, B—B1; 27. B—Q4, Q—Q1; 28. B—B4, with a similar constriction as in the game.

24. Q—N2   **P x P**
25. P—B5   **B—Q1**
26. P—Q6   **Q—B3**
27. Q x P   **K—R3**

Black is busily constructing a sort of sui-stalemate . Soon his pieces will not even be allowed standing room.

28. B—B4   **R—N2**
29. B—Q4   **Resigns.**

In fact, Truscott looked at me, drew up his shoulders and said: "Do you see a move? — I don't."

Game No. 11.

Improvisation of a basically new line of play in a well-established opening usually recoils on the improviser — at least where his opponent is of master or near-master strength. Yet the following game, from the international tournament at Saarbrücken 1953, shows that even in this scientific age it can still be done successfully. I do not know of any precursor of the completely unorthodox treatment of the Niemzo-Indian Defence in the following game; nor, I have to admit, does anybody seem to have copied it since. ("And not bloody likely either," I can hear the cynics comment.)

Black: O. Benkner.
Niemzo-Indian Defence.

1. P—Q4   **N—KB3**
2. P—QB4   **P—K3**
3. N—QB3   **B—N5**
4. P—K3   **P—B4**
5. B—Q3   **N—B3**
6. N—K2   **O—O**

7. P x P?!

This is the innovation played on the spur of the moment so as to get the game out of the books. The move is known from the Q—B2 (instead of P—K3) line of the Niemzo-Indian, where the QP is under attack, so that there is a tactical reason for the capture. Here the idea is purely strategic: Black is offered the "gift" of the two Bishops in exchange for pressure on the Q-file and developmental difficulties.

7. ...,	B x P
8. O—O	N—K4
9. P—QN3	P—QN3

Black wisely defers the capture of the B, giving White a chance to retract the offer.

10. B—N2	B—N2
11. N—R4	

Here I originally intended to withdraw the B and swap horses in midstream, but found that I am really committed. For if 11. B—B2, Black plays 11. ..., N(3)—N5! with the unpleasant threat of 12. ..., Q—R5; e.g. 12. P—KR3, Q—R5; 13. N—Q4, (13. PxN?, NxNP; with mate to follow), BxN; 14. QxB, N—B6ch; 15. PxN, BxP; 16. N—K2, P—K4!; and wins, or if 14. PxB, N—B6ch; 15. PxN, QxRP; and wins. Or again 13. N—K4, NxKP!; 14. PxN, BxPch; 15. N—B2, Q—N4; and wins. With the text White forces the acceptance of what Tarrasch used to call the "minor exchange".

11. ...,	N x B
12. Q x N	B—K2
13. QR—B1	Q—B2
14. N—N3	KR—Q1
15. N—B3	QR—B1
16. P—K4	

White's idea becomes clear: Black's QB is meant to "bite on granite' for the rest of the game and the freeing push P—Q4 is rendered impossible for a long time to come.

16. ...,   P—KR4?

A blunder, designed to remove one of the defenders of the KP which, however, reacts with the sort of violence to be expected from a startled horse. If Black tries to prepare for this move by, say, 16. ..., Q—N1; 17. Q—K2, poses new problems (P—Q4 is now impossible because of the indirect attack on Black's KB), while 16. ..., B—R3; is answered with 17. Q—B3. Black is certainly faced with difficult problems in exchange for his pair of Bishops.

17. N—N5	Q—B5
18. B x N	P x B

Hoping to save his material, but the two Knights co-operate too well.

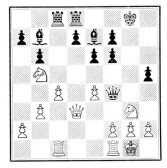

19. N x KRP	Q x KP
20. Q x Q	B x Q
21. N—Q6!	B x N
22. N x P ch	K—N2

If 22. ..., K—B1; the whole difference is that on move 25 White plays R—B3 instead of R—N3ch — he still clears square QB3 for the Knight.

23. N x B	B—R6
24. R—B3	P—B4
25. R—N3 ch	K—B2
26. N—B3	P—Q4

This in effect gives up a second pawn, but against quiet play the KRP is bound to win in the end. The rest is technique.

27. P x P	P x P
28. R—Q3	P—Q5

29. N—N5	B—N7
30. N x RP	R—B6
31. KR—Q1	R—QR1
32. N—N5	R x R
33. R x R	R x P
34. P—N3	R—R4
35. N—Q6 ch	K—K3
36. N—B4	

Recovering the second pawn. 35. ..., K—B3; would have made no difference because it would have allowed 39. N—Q5ch, instead of 39. N—R4.

36. ...,	R—R8 ch
37. K—N2	B—B6
38. N x P	R—N8
39. N—R4!	B—R8
40. K—B3	K—K4
41. K—K2	P—B5
42. P x P ch	K x P
43. R—Q1	R x P

Or 43. ..., RxR; 44. KxR, K—B6; 45. K—B2, K—K7!; 46. N—B5, KxP; 47. K—Q3, and the parallel advance of the white pawns cannot be stopped even though the B can creep out via QN7. Or 45. ..., P—Q6ch; 46. KxP, B—K4; 47. P—R4, KxP; 48. K—K4, and wins as above.

44. R x B	R—KR6
45. N—B5	Resigns.

The 45th was the sealed move, which White communicated to the opponent during the dinner adjournment. If now 45. ..., RxP; 46. N—Q3ch, K—K5; 47. R—R5, threatens mate on K5 and if Black "jokes" with 47. ..., R—R4 (48. RxR? stalemate), White has a little counter-joke: 48. P—B3 mate. "Well, if you compose problems . . ." the munching Dunkelblum said reproachfully.

Game No. 12.

"This bishop smiles. . . . The other bishop laughs heartily . . ." Lasker observes in his chapter on the aesthetic effect in chess (*Lasker's Manual of Chess*). There is a rich field for the comic and the amusing in chess — as there is in literature, painting, music, love-making and almost any human activity (I am not sure about atomic physics). Only those completely unreceptive to this sort of thing will not be tempted to smile at the spectacle of the black King, a refugee hunted from his hearth, shedding his disguise like a fairy prince and leading his shattered army to victory. In the end even the loser of the game cannot help joining in the general hilarity. In fact, the loser's smile widened to a broad grin when, many years later, this game (played in a small training match at Amsterdam 1954) was awarded the prize for the most amusing game in a competition run by Harry Golombek in the *Observer*.

Black: C. H. Roele.
Vienna Game.

1. P—K4	P—K4
2. N—QB3	N—KB3
3. P—B4	P—Q4
4. P x KP	N x P
5. P—Q3	N x N
6. P x N	B—K2

"Book" is 6. ..., P—Q5; followed by P—QB4. It will soon be seen that neither side is very ambitious in the opening.

7. N—B3	O—O
8. B—K2	

After Black has done without P—Q5 on the one hand, and is no longer able to go into Cortlever's dangerous line with P—QB4—B5, B—K3 and O—O—O on the other, it was certainly more logical to play 8. P—Q4 and thus enable the KB to go to Q3 in one move.

8. ...,	P—QB4
9. P—Q4	N—B3

10. O—O   P—B3
11. B—KB4   P—KN4

Amazingly enough, this wild move turns out well, though it is seriously to be doubted whether my opponent — or anybody else for that matter — would care to repeat the experiment.

12. P x KBP   P x B
13. P x B   Q x P
14. B—Q3   P—B5

Consistently suicidal!

15. R—K1   Q—R6

"Winning a pawn.' Needless to say, far from inviting it, my opponent had simply overlooked the coming sacrifice. He admitted after the game that by the time his K reached K5 he was ready to resign, playing on merely to see what would happen.

16. B x P ch   K x B
17. N—N5 ch!

White, who had sacrificed merely on "general principles" (HOW can so exposed a King survive the attack?), strikes the first snag. 17. N—K5, looks far more plausible, for neither 17. . . . , NxN?; nor 17. . . . , Q—Q3?; 18. NxN, would allow the black King to survive the assault of the white pieces. But Black would reply 17. . . . , K—R3!; letting the K conduct his own defence, and there seems to be no continuation of the attack.

17. . . . ,   K—N3
18. N—K6   B x N
19. R x B ch   K—B4

A reluctant dragon, the King is forced to invade enemy territory.

20. R—R6   Q x BP
21. Q—R5 ch   K—K5
22. R—Q1

Cutting off the King's escape via the Q-file and forcing the reply, for if 22. . . . , NxP?; 23. R—K6ch!, NxR; 24. QxPch, K—K6; 25. Q—B3 mate.

22. . . . ,   QR—K1
23. Q—N6 ch

This wins the black Queen. However, neither I nor my opponent had the foggiest notion that as a result of this material gain I would have to fight for the draw.

In view of the unsatisfactory sequel, the Dutch master, Carel J. van den Berg, suggested 23. R—Q6, NxP; 24. QxPch, K—K6; 25. K—B1, instead of the text. But then Black has the resource 25. . . . , R—B4! (to cut off the Queen from the K-side and prepare the advance of the KBP). This would force the sequel 26. QxN, with exchange of Queens and the superior endgame for Black, for if 26. QxNP?, Black wins with 26. . . . , P—B6!; 27. R(6)xN, PxP dbl ch; 28. K—N1 (or 28. KxP, R—N1ch; 29. K—R1, QxR!; 30. Q—K7ch, R—K4; 31. R—K1ch, K—B7), R—B8ch; 29. KxP, QxPch; 30. R(1)—Q2, R—N1ch; 31. KxR, Q—B4ch; 32. K—K1, R—N8 mate.

23. . . . ,   K—K6
24. R—R3 ch

Here Dr. Euwe took a hand in the post-mortem, suggesting 24. Q—K6ch (24. . . . , RxQ? ; 25. RxR and mate next move) but after 24. . . . , N—K4!; 25. QxP, K—K7!; 26. PxN, RxP; the black King shows himself supremely unimpressed.

24. . . . ,   P—B6!
25. R x P ch

34

Could, perhaps, the pin be exploited by stopping the black King at this particular point from journeying further? Thus 25. K—B1, NxP!; 26. Q—R6ch (if 26. Q—N5ch, so as to retain the possibility of a fatal check on KN1, Black would reply 26. ..., R—B5; 27. P—N3, N—K3!; 28. Q—R6, QxP; and wins, or 28. Q—R5, QxP; 29. Q—K5ch, R—K5; 30. R—K1ch, Q—K7ch! and wins), R—B5; 27. P—N3, R—K5; and though Black has to invest a whole Rook, the white King remains in the mating net woven largely by his colleague. No, the bird in the hand is decidedly better.

25. ...,	**K—K7**
26. R x Q	**K x R**
27. P—KR4?	

This ending of Q+P vs. R+N seems to be the best White could have obtained from his previous exertions, but now 27. P—KR3! would give better chances after 27. ..., NxP (obviously White could not both guard the mate and save his pawn); 28. R—Q3ch!, PxR; 29. QxPch, K—B8; 30. QxN. White would retain his two connected passed pawns without exposing his K, and he threatens to win a second pawn.

27. ...-,	**N x P**
28. K—R2?	

But this is a serious mistake (due to a disastrous underestimation of the opponent's counter-play). He should still have made the sacrifice of the previous note and if, at the end of it, 30. ..., R—K8ch; 31. K—R2, R—K5; he could try 32. Q—N1ch!, K—N7 (not 32. ..., KxP?; 33. Q—B5ch); 33. P—N3, while even 33. QxP, RxP ch; 34. K—N3 should be good enough for a draw. As he plays, he drifts into a loss.

28. ...,	**N—K7**
29. R—B3	**P—Q5**

30. P—R5	**R x R**
31. P x R	

So as to give the white King air to breathe, for if 31. QxR, R—K6; 32. Q—R4, P—B6; with the threat of 33. ..., P—Q6; whereas the white passed pawn cannot proceed (33. P—R6, R—K3!; threatening mate). Unfortunately the air for the white King is contaminated.

31. ...,	**R—K6**
32. Q—B5	

No better is 32. P—R6 (recommended in my book, *Chess Springbok*) because of 32. ..., RxP; 33. P—R7, R—R6 ch! (and not, as in the source quoted, 33. ..., R—B7ch?); 34. KxR, N—B5ch; 35. K—R4, NxQch; 36. K—N5, N—R1; 37. K—B6, P—Q6; 38. PxP, P—B6; 39. K—N7, P—B7; 40. KxN, P—B8(Q); and wins. This pretty line was found by a German amateur when the game was published in *Deutsche Schachzeitung*.

32. ...,	**P—Q6**
33. P x P	**P—B6**
34. Q—B5	**R x BP**
35. P—R6	**R—B3**
36. Q—KN5	**R—B7 ch**
37. K—R3	

Or 37. K—R1, P—B7; 38. P—R7, R—B1; 39. Q—N7, P—B8(Q); 40. QxR, K—Q7 dis ch; 41. K—N2, Q—N8ch; followed by mate or loss of the Queen.

37. ...,	**N—B5 ch**
38. K—N4	**R—N7 ch**
39. K—B5	

Ineffectually trying to hide behind the enemy piece.

39. ...,	**R x Q ch**
40. K x R	**P—B7**
41. P—R7	**P—B8(Q)**
42. P—R8(Q)	**N x P dis ch**
	Resigns.

Game No. 13.

As Spielmann was the first to point out, there are two kinds of sacrifice in chess. One is for gain (including the biggest gain, the hostile King) and must be calculated to the end, The other type of sacrifice is real instead of being made for gain. For all that it is an investment, and the investor expects to make a profit.

This profit, however, cannot be accurately calculated in advance. It consists in increased efficacy of the remaining units, control of important squares, lines and files, an exposed King (as e.g. in game No. 12) — in short, what is called "play". In a sense, all gambits are sacrifices of this kind: a pawn is offered for the sake of opening lines, increased mobility and, finally, the makings of an attack. But it is where the investment is more than a mere pawn (or at most a couple of pawns) that the thrill engendered by a "real" sacrifice makes itself felt: that the player commanding the depleted force sees his judgment (as distinct from his calculation) vindicated in the gradual increase in the power of his army till finally it triumphs over the opponent's stronger battalions. The following game, played in a small match at Utrecht 1954, is of this type.

White: E. Spanjaard.
Kings Indian Defence.

1. N—KB3	N—KB3
2. P—KN3	P—KN3
3. B—N2	B—N2
4. O—O	O—O
5. P—Q4	P—Q3
6. P—B4	QN—Q2
7. N—B3	P—K4
8. P—K3	

A quiet continuation aiming at strengthening the black squares in the centre. It is not without piquancy that the assault against these reinforced squares becomes the main theme of the game.

8. ...,	P—B3
9. Q—B2	R—K1
10. R—Q1	

It would have been better to develop the QB to R3 before occupying the Q-file and thus free the other Rook. The position of the QR will cause trouble later in the game.

10. ...,	Q—B2
11. P—N3	N—B1
12. B—QR3	P x P
13. N x P	B—N5
14. P—B3	

14. ...,	QR—Q1!(?)

The idea of Black's play. If White disregards the offer of the B, it would return to B1 after the black centre is fully protected. After long thought Spanjaard decided to take the piece, saying as he did so: "You have to show me!"

15. P x B	N x P
16. R—Q3	

With this move White decides to hold on to as much material as possible. The alternative was 16. P—K4, retaining two minor pieces for R + P; but once the KP has advanced it no longer contributes to the defence of the black squares, and White, with less material to the good, still is faced with essentially the same problem as in the game.

What now follows is not an "attack" — it is an attempt to exploit the black-squared weaknesses in the white camp, along the cross-roads QN3—KN8 and KN2—QR8. The basic idea is, of course, not new: it was presented in very attractive form in two famous games of Bronstein's (against Pachman and Zita) in the Moscow-Prague match 1946. But in those games Bronstein sacrificed for gain — here the sequel is quite incalculable.

16. ...,	N x KP
17. Q—Q2	Q—R4
18. B—N2	

If 18. RxN, B—R3; but in any case White is glad to be able to strengthen the long diagonal.

| 18. ..., | N—N5 |

This quiet retreat came as a surprise to White. It retains all existing threats and creates a few more (B—R3).

19. N—K4!

Active defence, which sooner or later threatens a Queen sacrifice if Black plays the B to R3. On the other hand, White can no longer play N—QR4 to drive away the black Queen from N3 from where it adds to the pressure on the unhappy Knight. Moreover, as the game shows, the N on K4 will itself become a target for Black's attack and should therefore have regarded K4 merely as a port of call instead of a permanent abode (see following note).

| 19. ..., | Q—N3 |
| 20. K—R1? | |

This instinctive unpin is the decisive mistake. Much better was Dr. Euwe's suggestion, 20. N—B2! If then 20. ..., B—R3?; 21. NxN!, BxQ; 22. N—B6ch, K—R1; 23. RxB, with, for the time being, three minor pieces for Queen and two pawns — but the certainty of winning at least another ex-change.

With 20. ..., B—R3?; out of the question, and assuming that White declines the repetition of moves which is available to him in the following line, best play for both sides would probably run: 20. ..., N—K4; 21. R—QB3, N—N5; 22. R—B2! (not 22. R(3)—B1? because, with the white Queen unprotected, 22. ..., B—R3; could no longer be answered with 23. NxN), N—K6; 23. R(2)—B1, R—K2; with the idea of doubling Rooks on the K-file. White would then still be a long way from shaking off the pressure, though the position resists a precise analysis.

| 20. ..., | P—Q4! |
| 21. P x P | |

White has no choice, for if 21. P—B5?, Q—R3!; threatening 22. ..., PxN. If the N moves, there would follow 22. ..., QxRch; 23. QxQ, N—B7ch — the result of White's error on move 20. But now the black QR participates in the battle against the Knight — and that proves too much.

| 21. ..., | R x P |
| 22. Q—B4 | |

A clever resource, so as to punish 22. ..., N—K4?; with 23. N—B6ch, BxN; 24. QxB, NxR; 25. BxR! (not the "clever" 25. N—B5? because of 25. ..., N—B7ch), PxB; 26. N—K6! with unanswerable mate.

| 22. ..., | R x N(Q5)! |
| 23. R—KB1 | |

Black threatened 23. ..., R(5)xN; 24. BxR, RxB; 25. QxR, N—B7ch; and if 23. BxR, BxB; 24. RxB, QxR; he would be two pawns up with an easily-won game.

23. ...,	P—KB4
24. B x R	B x B
25. P—KR3	N—K3

The decisive call-up of the reserves. Meanwhile Black, with two pawns for the exchange, has equalized material.

26. Q—B3	N—K4
27. N—B6 ch	K—B2
28. N—Q5?	

A pity that White, with 13 moves to complete in less than two minutes, spoils his game completely. However, he was lost even without this over-sight. Best was 28. NxR!, NxQ; 29. N—Q6ch, when Black will have the Queen and one extra pawn on each wing for the two Rooks.

28. ...,	P x N
29. Q x P	N x R

and White resigned shortly after.

Game No. 14.

Queenless middle games producing lively combinational turns exert a peculiar fascination. They occur infrequently — among the great masterpieces of chess literature I can recall only three examples off-hand: Takacs-Rubinstein, Rogaska Slatina 1929, Pleci-Endzelius, Buenos Aires 1939, and the breath-taking draw in the 7th game of the Schlechter-Lasker match.

Naturally the following game, played in the South African championship at Cape Town 1955, cannot stand comparison with such illustrious fore-runners. But nobody can deny that it contains an unusual amount of involved play off the beaten track.

Black: M. Bennett.
Sicilian Defence.

1. P—K4	P—QB4
2. P—QB3	P—Q3
3. P—Q4	N—KB3(?)

A careless move, which virtually forces Black to seek complications at this early stage.

4. P x P!

This simple reply poses Black serious positional problems. He cannot play 4. ..., NxP?; because 5. Q—R4ch would cost a piece. 4. ..., PxP; 5. QxQch, KxQ; would leave him with poor prospects because his QBP has already moved to B4. Generally, it may be said that all lines involving an early KxQ (as e.g. the Old Indian) are playable only because the centre can be held (and frequently the K, forced to emigrate to QB2, sheltered) by the move P—QB3.

A game Heidenfeld - Grzeskowiak, Frankfurt/Main 1960, which continued with 4. ..., PxP; 5. QxQch, KxQ; 6. P—B3, N—B3; 7. B—QB4, P—K3; 8. N—KR3, B—Q2; 9. B—K3, N—K4(?); 10. B—K2, B—K2; 11. N—Q2, P—KR3; 12. N—B2, P—KN4; 13. N—N3, P—QN3; 14. O—O—O, spot-lights the difficulties Black encounters in the type of game apt to arise from 4. ..., PxP. Bennett obviously dis-liked these prospects so much that he decided to offer an interesting gambit.

4. ...,	N—B3!?
5. P x P	N x P
6. P x P	Q x Q ch
7. K x Q	B x P

After 7. ..., NxPch; 8. K—K1, NxR; 9. PxB(Q)ch, RxQ; the black Knight will eventually be lost. After the text move Black is a pawn down but has three developed pieces against none; and since White can no longer castle, Black will bring out his Rooks more swiftly and efficiently than his opponent. Yet this advantage is largely nullified by the absence of Queens and also by the central power of the white QBP, which controls a central square no longer open to attack by a hostile pawn.

8. B—K3	B—K3
9. N—B3	

Played after half an hour's reflec-tion. It is tempting to kick the Knight by P—B3 (reserving square KB2 for the King at the same time), but the temptation must be withstood, as the development of the King-side pieces would have presented great difficulties. First the white Knight must be brought to the strong square Q4. Another illustration of the principle that the acceptor of a gambit must sacrifice positional desiderata to rapid development.

9. ...,	R—Q1 ch
10. K—K1	O—O
11. QN—Q2	N—B4
12. N—Q4	B—Q4
13. P—B3	KR—K1
14. K—B2	

Now White has achieved the desired formation. If Black pursues a slow build-up, his lead in development will soon disappear, e.g. 14. ..., N—K4; 15. B—QN5, or 14. ..., B—B3; 15. N(2)—N3. Bennett therefore conceives an ingenious exchange sacrifice which, though not correct in the last analysis, may well be his best practical chance.

14. ...,	B—R5 ch
15. P—N3	R x B?!
16. K x R	B—N4 ch
17. K—K2	R—K1 ch

Of course not 17. ..., BxN?; 18. KxB, BxBP; 19. KR—N1, NxN; 20. PxN, RxPch; 21. K—K3! when Black is forced to 21. ..., R—Q8; 22. RxR, BxR; 23. B—N2, which would leave him nothing to play for.

| 18. K—Q1 | N—K4 |
| 19. P—QB4 | |

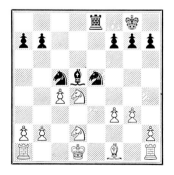

I remember getting up after this move and remarking to an expert on-looker "First things first!". The reference is to the fact that the text returns the exchange but, in doing so, keeps a powerful extra pawn. Trying to preserve all the material would be positionally feeble: 19. B—N5, R—Q1; 20. R—K1, NxP; 21. N(2)xN, BxNch; 22. B—K2 (otherwise Black has perpetual check or recovers the exchange), B—K5!; and White will find it difficult to disentangle his pieces. Or, in this line, 20. R—KB1, BxN; 21. KxB, BxP; 22. K—K3, B—N7; 23. R—B5, P—B3; with an unclear position (24. P—QN4 can be answered with 24. ..., P—KN3; 25. R—B4, P—KN4; 26. R—B5, N—N5ch, etc.)

| 19. ..., | N—N5! |

Yet another surprising twist. It is tragic for Black that each of these flashes of ingenuity brings White one step nearer the ending he has in mind.

| 20. P x B | N—B7 ch |

(20. ..., N—K6ch; 21. K—B1, R—QB1; 22. K—N1.)

| 21. K—B2 | N x R |
| 22. B—N5 | |

This does NOT win a piece as might appear at first glance. Again Black has made adequate provision.

| 22. ..., | R—QB1 |
| 23. R x N | N—K3 dis ch! |

But not 23. ..., N—K5 dis ch?; 24. N—B4, N—B7; 25. R—KB1, B—K6; 26. N—B5 and wins.

24. K—Q3	N x N
25. K x N	B x N
26. R—Q1	B—N5
27. K—K5!	K—B1?

Black has to prevent P—Q6 at all costs and should have played 27. ..., P—QR3!; 28. P—QR3, B—B1; 29. B—R4, P—QN4; 30. B—N3, R—K1 ch; 31. K—Q4, when he might have held the ending. Now the opposite-coloured Bishops disappear and the white R gets to the 7th rank.

28.	B—R4	K—K2
29.	P—Q6 ch	K—Q1
30.	P—QR3!	R—B4 ch

For if 30. ..., B—R4; 31. P—QN4, B—N3; 32. K—Q5, threatening 33. R—K1, and 34. R—K8 mate.

31.	K—Q4	R—QR4
32.	P x B	R x B
33.	K—B5	R—R3
34.	R—K1	R—B3 ch
35.	K—Q5	R—B7
36.	R—K7	

Here the game was adjourned — appropriately enough, for it is an organic and aesthetic whole up to this point. With the white Rook on the 7th — where it menaces no fewer than five pawns — the fight is over and Black might well have saved himself the following agony:

36. ..., R—Q7ch; 37. K—B5, R—B7ch; 38. K—N5, K—B1; 39. RxBP, RxNP; 40. R—B7ch, K—N1; 41. Rx KNP, P—R3ch; 42. K—B5, RxRP; 43. K—N6, K—B1; 44. RxNP, R—R3; 45. R—B7ch, K—Q1; 46. K—B6, Resigns.

Game No. 15.

To beat a player who has held the world championship — even though twenty years before — cannot help being a high-water mark in the career of an untitled woodshifter. This game, played in the penultimate round of the international tournament at Johannesburg 1955, helped me to come up from the ruck and force a dead-heat with Mühring, half a point ahead of the former world champion.

Black: Dr. M. Euwe.
Giuoco Piano.

1.	P—K4	P—K4
2.	N—KB3	N—QB3
3.	B—B4	B—B4
4.	P—B3	B—N3
5.	P—Q4	Q—K2
6.	O—O	P—Q3
7.	P—KR3	N—B3
8.	R—K1	O—O
9.	P—QR4	P—QR3
10.	N—R3	

An attempt to combine the "classic" system (P—QR4, P—QN4) with that of Rossolimo (N—R3 with the double threat of N—B4 and N—B2—K3—Q5). As White plays, he does not really test his new idea, the most significant feature of which is the vacation of square QR2 for the retreat of the white Bishop. Thus a game Heidenfeld-Littleton, Dublin League 1968, continued with 10. ..., P—R3; 11. B—R2, B—R2; 12. N—B4, R—K1;

13. N—K3, Q—Q1; and now 14. Q—N3! (instead of the ill-considered 14. P—Q5?) would have posed difficult problems.

10.	...,	K—R1
11.	N—B2	N—KN1
12.	P—QN4	P—B3
13.	N—K3	B—R2
14.	B—R3	Q—K1
15.	Q—Q3	

In the fashion characteristic of this difficult variation Black has anticipated all potential threats before they materialise. Thus there is no point (at this stage!) in playing N—Q5, which would be answered with B—N1 whereupon Black would stand ready to attack White's central structure on both wings, by P—QB3 and P—KB4 (as, with wings and pawn moves interchanged, often happens in the French Defence). The Q move is designed to support a number of points that have to be maintained — QN5, K4, KB5

40

and, on occasion, KR3.

15. ...,	QN—K2
16. P—N5	P x NP
17. P x NP	Q—R4

My opponent later advocated 17. ..., N—N3; as better, but after 18. N—Q5, B—N1; 19. B—N4, White seems to have excellent prospects. The Q-move (threatening BxRP) forces the white Knight to retire to B1 and may thus well be worth the expenditure of a tempo.

| 18. N—B1 | Q—K1 |

If now 18. ..., N—N3; 19. N—N3, Q—R3; 20. B—B1, will leave the black Queen poorly placed.

| 19. R—K2 | N—N3? |

Black is so set on getting this move in that he commits a terrible oversight. After the correct move, 19. ..., B—N3; White would have played 20. R(2)—R2, N—N3; 21. B—N4, RxR; 22. RxR, N—B5; 23. Q—N1, with the idea of exchanging the black-squared Bishops by B—R5 and then entering on the QR-file, to counter-balance Black's incipient attack on the other wing. This would have led to a full-bodied fight with chances for both sides.

| 20. B—B1 | B—Q2 |
| 21. R(2)—R2 | Q—N1 |

The only move to save the piece for the time being. It is not without piquancy that six years later I got into an almost identical mess (from quite a different opening) against Czerniak

(compare game No. 31).

22. P—N6!

Systematic containment of the immobilised Bishop. The three pieces in the North-West corner are now tied together permanently and White need not worry about surprise sorties such as would have occurred after the "winning" move whispered audibly by the spectators: 22. PxP?, BPxP; 23. B—K3, P—N3; 24. B—Q5. For Black would not have played 22. ..., BPxP?, but 22. ..., NxP!; 23. NxN, BPxN; 24. B—K3, BxB!; 25. RxR, BxPch; 26. K—R1, QxR; 27. RxQ, RxR; — and with R, B and P for the Queen there is no earthly reason why Black should lose.

A perfectly good alternative, however, was suggested by Dr. Euwe: 22. B—K3. If then 22. ..., N—B5?; 23. QBxN, PxB; 24. BxN, and White cannot be stopped from trebling pieces (with the Queen *behind* one of the Rooks) on the QR-file. Better for Black would be 22. ..., P—KB4!; 23. PxKP, BPxP; 24. QxP, B—KB4; 25. Q—Q5, N(1)—K2; 26. Q any, P—N3; and the win is no quicker than in the text.

22. ...,	P x NP
23. B—QN5	B x B
24. Q x B	N(1)—K2
25. N—K3	N—B1
26. N—Q5	N(3)—K2
27. N x N	N x N
28. P x P!	

The fatal opening of the game. If now 28. ..., QPxP; 29. B—R3, is obviously decisive. If 28. ..., BPxP; 29. B—K3! (stronger than the immediate 29. N—N5, N—B3!; which I might have played), N—B1; 30. N—N5 (stopping Q—B2 and threatening an eventual smothered mate after Q—Q5), P—R3; 31. N—K6, R—N1; 32. Q—Q7, and the black pieces have to watch helplessly from their corners as the cheeky Knight threatens N—B7.

28. ...,	N—B3
29. P x QP	N—R4
30. B—R3	R—Q1
31. P—K5	Q—B1
32. B—N4	N—B3

The relief troops have to be called back. If, instead, 32. ..., N—N6; 33. RxB, NxR; 34. RxR, QxR; 35. P—K6, and the pawns are unstoppable.

33. Q—Q5	P x P
34. N x P	N x N

35. Q x N

As we were. Now there are no more relief troops.

35. ...,	Q—N1
36. Q—K7	P—QN4

and resigned at the same time, for there is no defence against 37. RxB.

At the time this game caused a sensation in South Africa; it even became the subject of one of the questions in Eric Rosenthal's *South African Quiz Book!*

Game No. 16.

Played at the international tournament at San Benedetto del Tronto 1956, this game was awarded a brilliancy prize. Admittedly White offers no more than a pawn as far as material is concerned (though there is the hidden offer of a piece in the variation given at Black's 21st move). However, in the words of the adjudicator, the award was made for the manner in which White, after the stormy opening, never allowed the opponent to catch his breath throughout the game.

Black: Dr. J. Fricker.

French Defence, Alapin Gambit.

1. P—K4	P—K3
2. P—Q4	P—Q4
3. B—K3	P x P
4. P—KB3	N—KB3
5. P x P	N x P
6. B—Q3	

If now 6. ..., Q—R5ch?; 7. P—N3, NxP; 8. B—B2, wins a piece. But the possibility of this check fascinates Black and induces him to disregard positional requirements. The best continuation of this rarely-played gambit is the modest retreat, 6. ..., N—KB3; 7. N—KB3, when White has about the equivalent of 1½ moves in development plus possession of the open KB-file for his pawn — which may just not be quite enough.

6. ...,	N—Q2?
7. Q—B3	

Of course not 7. BxN, Q—R5ch.

7. ...,	P—KB4

Naturally Black is not enamoured of the re-developing move 7. ...,

N(5)—B3 at this stage, though this would have been the lesser evil. Some years ago the *South African Chessplayer* hailed this move as a "refutation"of White's line of play on the strength of a game, Friedgood-Snoek, in which White made one anti-gambit move after another and quickly lost. After 7. ..., N(5)—B3; 8. KN—R3!, P—B4; 9. N—B3!, PxP; 10. BxP, White has an enormous edge in development (on e.g. 10. ..., P—K4?; White could already give up a piece by 10. O—O!, PxB; 11. QR—K1ch; B—K2; 12. N—Q5) and has certainly full compensation for his pawn.

8. N—Q2	N—N4

Black seems to have overlooked that he cannot keep the N on its commanding outpost — the purpose for which he made the inferior moves N—Q2 and P—KB4 — for 8. ..., N(2)—B3; would allow 9. BxN, NxB; 10. NxN, Q—R5ch; 11. N—B2.

9. Q—N3	B—K2
10. B—KB4	N—K5

So as to answer 11. BxP with NxQ and 11. BxN with B—R5. But now the white Queen gets into Black's innards.

11. Q x P	B—B3
12. Q—R6	N x N
13. B x N	

13. KxN had to be considered, but after 13. ..., N—B1; to be followed by QxP or P—B4 Black gets as much play on the Q-file as White does on the K-file.

13. ...,	B x P
14. N—K2	

After 14. QxPch, Q—K2; 15. BxP, White would clearly have the better game, but there is no urgency about this. For if now 15. ..., BxP; White can always fall back on 15. QxPch, Q—K2; 16. QxQch, KxQ; 17. R—N1, B any; 18. BxP, with some positional advantage. Meanwhile Black has to calculate the consequences of a further pawn sacrifice (14. ..., BxP; 15. R—N1, with a massive lead in development) and even lines in which White might give up his QR for the sake of a storming attack. Under a time limit it is clearly advantageous for White to let the opponent stew in his own juice.

14. ...,	B—B3
15. O—O—O	N—K4
16. Q—R5 ch	N—B2
17. B—N4!	

Holding the black King and threatening B—N5ch.

17. ...,	B—Q2
18. KR—K1	

Obviously Black won't be able to stand the battering along the central files much longer. He therefore prepares for O—O—O, but there is a snag.

18. ...,	P—QR4
19. B—R3	B—N4 ch
20. K—N1	Q—B3

This shows why 18. ..., P—QR4; was a necessary preliminary to O—O—O: White must not be able to play B—B3 in this position, but:

21. Q—B3!

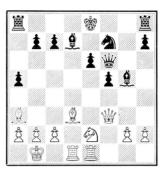

21. ...,	B—B3

Alas, he realizes that he cannot get the King away after all. For if now 21. ..., O—O—O; 22. B—R6, P—B3; 23. BxPch!, KxB; 24. Q—N3ch. Now the black King must not go to the R-file, for if 24. ..., K—R1; 25. Q—N6, followed by 26. B—B5, with unanswerable mate; and if 24. ..., K—R3; 25. Q—B4ch, followed by R—Q3—N3. The K must therefore return to the B-file: (a) 25. ..., K—B2; 26. B—B5, R—QN1; 27. Q—R3, R—N4; 28. P—B4, RxB; 29. QxR, with the double threat of N—Q4 and Q—R7ch (e.g. 29. ..., R—QN1; 30. Q—R7ch, R—N2; 31. RxBch, followed by 32. QxRch), or (b) 25. ..., K—B1; 26. Q—N6, B—K1 (if 26. ..., Q—K4; 27. Q—R6ch, K—B2; 28. N—Q4); 27. N—Q4, P—K4; 28. Q—R6ch, K—B2; 29. QxRPch, K—B1; 30. Q—R6ch, K—B2; 31. Q—R7ch, K—B1; 32. R—Q3!, RxN; 33. R—N3, with unanswerable mate. Although in all these variations the white pieces have to be brought to the attack from far afield, their black counter-parts are in such a tangle that they cannot parry the threats as they arise.

22. B—N5!	N—K4
23. Q—QN3	K—B2
24. N—Q4	B—Q4

25. Q—N3

Forcing Black to expose the neuralgic spot, his K3, still further.

25. ...,   P—B5
26. Q—R3   P—B3?

This loses horribly. White's principal threat—not an obvious one—was 27. N—B5! with the further threat of 28. B—K7 if the Knight is not captured. On the capture, 27. ..., QxN; 28. QxQ, PxQ; 29. RxB, the black game dissolves into its component parts. With the text Black therefore tries to support his B and also to gain time for QR—K1, but overlooks that White need not move the attacked B. Since 26. ..., N—N3; 27. P—B4, would allow the white pieces to enter the black game like a spring tide, there remains only 26. ..., QR—Q1; 27. RxN!, QxR; 28. Q—R5ch, K—N2 (if 28. ..., K—B3; 29. P—KR4); 29. B—K7, B—B3; 30. QxQ, BxQ; 31. BxR, and now (a) 31. ..., RxB; 32. NxPch, BxN; 33. RxR, winning the exchange — the white R cannot be cut off by 33. ..., B—Q3; because of 34. B—Q7, B—K2; 35. R—QB8!, BxB; 36. RxP. Or (b) 31. ..., BxN; 32. BxP, R—QB1 (32. ..., P—K4; 33. BxPch, BxB; 34. RxB, would allow

opposite-coloured Bishops, but at the expense of two pawns); 33. RxB, RxB; 34. RxP, which leaves White with an extra pawn and easy targets in the isolated black pawns.

27. B—Q6!   N—B5

In the hope of 28. BxN, BxB; 29. B—K5, Q—N3; 30. BxR, etc., when the two well-placed black Bishops might still give a lot of trouble. In any case he had little choice since 27. ..., N—N3; 28. P—B4, PxB; 29. PxB, PxP; 30. Q—Q7ch, would be hopeless.

28. B x N   B x B
29. N—B3!

Threatening one Bishop by Q—R5ch, the other by N—K5ch, while the exchange still remains *en prise*. In the sequel White refuses to pick up the material on offer, forcing the opponent to swap off pieces for fear of increasingly heavy losses. In the resultant final position mate is forced in a few moves.

29. ...,   B—Q4
30. Q—R5 ch   K—N1
31. B—K5   B x N
32. P x B   Q—N3
33. Q—R3   B—B3
34. Q x KP ch   Resigns.

Game No. 17.

Tal has shown in many games, even against his fellow grandmasters, that chess can be a slugging game, virtually without long-range planning and completely governed by the trading of punches; no strategy and all tactics. It works, even at a very high level, as long as the catch-as-catch-canner's imagination is more fertile than that of his opponent — if only to the extent that the other man, in meeting all the slings and arrows of his outrageous opponent, runs foul of his clock, This may not happen often at the top, but further down the chess scale the number of punch-traders increases. One of the most imaginative players of this type is D. Horseman, whom I met in the second round of the British Championship at Blackpool, 1956:

White: D. Horseman.
French Defence.

1. P—K4   P—K3
2. P—Q3   P—Q4

3. N—Q2   N—Q2

A non-committal move, which cannot be bad: a Knight is generally well-placed on Q2 where the opponent's QP does duty on Q3 rather than Q4. If White now changes plans and tries to exploit the position of the black N by a deferred P—Q4, Black brings about the Rubinstein variation (PxKP) with a move in hand.

4. P—KB4

We are already out of the books and it is each for himself now.

4. . . . ,	P x P
5. P x P	B—B4
6. KN—B3	KN—B3
7. P—K5	N—Q4
8. N—K4	Q—K2

I felt it was more important to develop quickly in this position than to retain the pair of Bishops. My opponent seems to concur, for he does not bother to pick up the Bishop either here or later and finally exchanges it for his own Bishop.

9. P—QR3	O—O
10. P—B4	N—K6
11. Q—Q3	N x B
12. R x N	P—QR4
13. P—KN4	P—B4

Surprising, but fully justified in this position. The white pawn roller is stopped before it has time to gather speed. If now 14. PxP e.p. Black would continue in the same style with 14. . . . , PxP?!

14. P x P

White has different ideas. He wants to remove the black KP from the protection of square Q5, thus force Black to guard this square by P—QB3 and then enter on Q6. Black, of course, will not be inactive.

14. . . . ,	P x P
15. N—B3	P—B3
16. B—K3	B x B
17. Q x B	N—B4!

At the time I thought that Black should have played 17. . . . , Q—B4; since it is clear that after the exchange of Queens Black could exploit the opponent's pawn weaknesses. But with 18. Q—Q4! White could leave the

onus of exchanging to Black and obtain much the better game.

18. R—Q1	B—K3
19. R—Q6	P—QN3
20. N—Q4	B x P!

Black, too, knows no fear.

21. N x QBP	Q—QB2
22. R—N1	QR—K1
23. Q—Q4	

Guarding against the threat of 23. . . . , QxR; and threatening 24. QxBch. But Black would not dream of removing his well-placed Bishop.

23. . . . ,	K—R1!

24. K—Q1

This allows Black a pretty coup. 24. P—N4, is pointless since the black N can safely go to N6—if White then plays QxB, Black takes the R and though his N then hangs, so does the white N on B6. Thus the only worthwhile alternative would have been 24. K—B2, B—K3; 25. N—N5, Q—B2; and Black threatens both Q—R4 and N—K5ch. Or 25. P—N4, PxP; 26. PxP, N—N2; and again White's seemingly strong position does not yield anything.

24. . . . ,	B—N6 ch
25. K—B1	B—R5!
26. Q—Q5	

He has to guard against both N—N6ch and BxN.

26. . . . ,	B—N6
27. Q—Q4	

The alternative was 27. Q—N2, but with little time left even my intrepid opponent shuddered at the vision of the witches' cauldron ahead, e.g. 27. ..., N—K5!; 28. N—N5, Q—B2; 29. R—Q3 (if 29. R—Q4, R—B1), B—B5! (if now 29. ..., R—B1; 30. RxB!, RxNch; 31. K—N1, N—Q7ch; 32. QxN, QxR; 33. N—Q4); 30. N—Q6, BxR!; 31. NxQch, RxN; and now either —

(a) 32. N—Q4, R—B2ch; 33. K—Q1, R—Q1 (naturally the R moves along the first and second ranks cannot be interchanged); 34. N—K6, B—B8 dis ch; 35. NxR, BxQ; 36. RxB, R—Q2ch; and wins a piece; or

(b) 32. R—Q1, R—Q2; 33. Q—B3, N—B4; 34. P—N4, B—K5; 35. RxR, BxQ; 36. PxN, BxN; 37. R—QB7, B—Q4! (guarding back-rank mating threats); 38. PxP, R—QN1; and Black retains his extra piece; or

(c) 32. Q—B3, B—N4; 33. N—Q4, R—B2ch; 34. N—B2, R(1)—QB1; 35. R—N2, B—R5; 36. P—N3, R—B6; and wins.

Or, on a completely different tack:

28. NxN, PxN; 29. Q—N3! (29. QxP?, QxR), P—K6!; 30. K—N1, P—KN4; 31. QxNP (if 31. N—Q4, PxP), P—K7! (threatening 32. ..., P—K8(Q)ch; 33. RxQ, QxR); 32. Q—R4 (if 32. Q—N3, R—KN1; if 32. R—Q2, P—K8 (Q)ch; 33. RxQ, QxN), RxBP!; 33. Q—K1, B—B5!; 34. R—B6, RxR; 35. PxR, QxN and wins. These are mere "specimens" of play, and White may be able to do better, but — tactician or not — would *you*, with time running out, have played 27. Q—N2?

27. ...,	B—R5
28. Q—Q5	B—N6
29. Q—Q4	

Drawn by repetition of moves.

Since eventually I did not distinguish myself in this tournament and the half-point one way or the other would have meant very little to either my opponent or myself, I cannot, in retrospect, help regretting that the scrap sketched in merest outline in the previous note, did not actually materialize.

Game No. 18.

I have had a lot of fun with the R sacrifice variation of the Alekhine-Chatard attack in the French, breaking about even in the process. In the following game, played in the British Championship at Blackpool, 1956, White tries to improve on the "book", but even the wobbly "book" of so dubious a line is not easily improved.

White: A. R. B. Thomas.

French Defence.

1. P—K4	P—K3
2. P—Q4	P—Q4
3. N—QB3	N—KB3
4. B—N5	B—K2
5. P—K5	KN—Q2

In recent years I have preferred the interesting Niemzovich line, 5. ..., N—N1 (see games Nos. 43 and 47).

| 6. P—KR4 | P—QB4 |
| 7. B x B | Q x B?! |

Here 7. ..., KxB; is perfectly playable and circumvents the following sacrifice.

| 8. N—N5 | O—O |

And here 8. ..., K—Q1; might be worth a try.

| 9. N—B7 | P x P |
| 10. B—Q3? | |

This is Thomas' new idea: he wants to answer an eventual Q—N5ch with K—B1 instead of the usual Q—Q2 and thus avoid having the QR attacked after QxNP. However, the white B gets into the path of the advancing black pawns and the innovation is clearly inferior to the normal 10. NxR

46

with the possibilities, 10. ..., P—B3; 11. QxP, N—B3 (as in Bronstein-Stahlberg, Budapest 1950); or 10. ..., N—B3; 11. N—B3, Q—N5ch; 12. Q—Q2, QxP; 13. R—Q1, N—B4; 14. B—Q3, B—Q2; 15. N—B7, R—B1; 16. NxQP! After many experiences in this line I now believe that the generally accepted verdict, "slight plus for White" is correct.

10. ...,	**N—QB3**
11. N x R	**N(2) x P**
12. N—B3	**N x B ch**

When the game was played, this B looked dangerous to me, but in retrospect I would certainly opt for 12. ..., NxNch; and if then 13. QxN, P—K4!; 14. QxQP, B—K3; to be followed by RxN, with a wonderfully dynamic position for the small material minus (N+P vs. R). As played, White gets good service out of his Knight.

13. Q x N	**P—K4**
14. Q—R3!	**Q—Q1!**
15. O—O	

White wants to avoid the pin of his N in case a white R appears on Q1. He therefore threatens to sacrifice his KN against a black centre pawn and then free his other N by QxRP. Black would then be the exchange down with nothing to show for it. However, the weakness of the white KRP (one of the *raisons d'etre* of this whole method of play) enables Black to put a stop to this little scheme.

15. ...,	**P—K5**
16. N—Q2	

For if 16. NxP?, NxN; 17. QxP, N—K7ch; followed by QxP mate.

16. ...,	**B—K3**
17. N—N3	**Q x N**
18. QR—Q1!	

With this and the next move White succeeds in breaking up the black centre pawns. This could not be achieved by 18. Q—B5?, P—QN3!; or 18. Q—R4, P—QR3! 19. NxP?, P—QN4).

18. ...,	**B—N5**
19. P—KB3!	

As planned. After 19. R—Q2, the game would have become very complicated. My own suggestion at the time, 19. ..., Q—Q1; 20. NxP, N—K4 (threatening to win the Rook by N—B5 and thus "forcing" P—QN3, which would cut off the white Queen) is inadequate because of 21. Q—KN3!, N—B5; 22. QxB, NxR; 23. R—Q1, N—B5; 24. N—B5, P—KN3; 25. RxP! Black would therefore have to play 19. ..., P—K6; 20. PxP, PxP; 21. RxP, and now not (as recommended in several columns) the immediate 21. ..., P—K7; 22. R—K1, but first 21. ..., R—Q1! The difference lies in the fact that, with the P prematurely on K7, White could dig his R in with P—B4; when the P is still on K6, this could be answered with B—K3. After, e.g. 21. ..., R—Q1!; 22. Q—B5, P—K7; 23. R—K1, RxR; 24. QxR, Q—K1; Black's passed pawn would be worth at least the exchange.

19. ...,	**P x P**
20. P x P	**B—R6**
21. R—B2	**Q—Q1**
22. N x P	**Q x P**
23. N—K2	

Not the losing move, though it makes the defence more difficult. Strongest was 23. Q—K3 with the likely sequel, 23. ..., Q—N6ch (if 23. ..., P—B4; 24. R—R2, P—B5; 25. Q—K6ch!); 24. K—R1, P—B4; 25. R—R2, P—B5; with about even chances. Out of the question would be 23. NxN?, Q—N6ch; 24. K—R1, QxR; 25. N—K7ch, K—R1; 26. N—N6ch, RPxN; 27. QxRch, K—R2; 28. R—KN1, B—B8! and White can stop mate only by 29. RxB, remaining three pawns down.

23. ...,	**R—K1**
24. Q—Q6?	

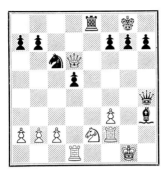

This finds an almost problem-like refutation. Broadbent recommends 24. RxP!, when 24. ..., R—K3; 25. P—B4! (so as to answer 25. ..., R—N3ch with 26. R—N5), P—KR3; 26. R—Q3!, B—B4; 27. R—K3, B—K5; 28. N—N3, R—N3; can be answered with 29. K—B1! Black therefore should make sure of the draw by answering 25. P—B4, with 25. ..., RxN!; 26. RxR, Q—N5ch; and now (a) 27. K—B2, Q—N7ch; 28. K—K1 (28. K—K3?, QxR), Q—R8ch! and

draw by perpetual check since the K must not enter the Q-file; or (b) 27. K—R1 (not, of course, 27. K—R2?, QxRch; 28. KxB, Q—K3ch), QxR; 28. QxB, Q—K5ch; 29. Q—N2, Q—K8ch; and Black has the choice between picking up pawns and taking the perpetual.

	24. ...,	R—K4!

This intersecting move required courage as well as calculation—in the previous round I had lost a "won game" against Barden by allowing a snap mate on the back rank. I certainly made trebly sure that the same thing would not happen again.

25. R—R2	R—N4 ch
26. K—R1	B—N7 ch
27. K—N1	B x P dis ch
28. K—B1	B x N ch
Resigns.	

If 29. KxB, R—K4ch; 30. QxR, Q—N5ch; 31. any, NxQ; or 29. RxB, R—B4ch; 30. K—N2, Q—N5ch; and White loses all his goods and chattels.

Game No. 19.

"It serves me right," my opponent said after resigning the following game at the Paignton tournament 1956. He was referring to his passive play, which left him with a "book" ending of bad vs. good Bishop, aggravated by the presence of one Rook each and the resultant combinational possibilities.

White: R. H. Newman.

Dutch Defence (in effect).

1. P—QB4	P—KB4
2. N—KB3	N—KB3
3. P—KN3	P—Q3
4. P—Q4	P—KN3

The so-called Leningrad variation — dubious where White has refrained from P—QB4, but full value in the present position. One may say that wherever 1. P—QB4 has been answered with a Dutch set-up White does better to allow the P—KB4—K4—Q3 configuration and play P—Q3 rather than P—Q4.

5. B—N2	B—N2
6. N—B3	O—O
7. O—O	N—B3
8. P—Q5	N—K4
9. N x N	P x N
10. P—K4	P—K3
11. B—N5	

If 11. PxKP, P—B3; and Black recovers the pawn with a good hold on the centre squares. The text gives White nothing at all.

11. ...,	P x QP
12. N x P	

Leading to a simplification greatly in Black's favour.

12. ...,	P—B3
13. N x N ch	B x N

14. Q x Q	**B x Q**
15. B x B	**R x B**
16. KR—Q1	**B—K3**

Black has a tempo advantage in addition to the better Bishop. It is clear that square Q5 will ultimately be a black strong point, unless White takes immediate measures against it.

17. P—N3	**K—B2**

The immediate 17. ..., P—B5; would be premature: 18. PxP, PxP; 19. P—B5, K—B2 (if 19. ..., B—N5; 20. R—Q6, P—B6?; 21. P—KR3!); 20. R—Q6. But White must keep this possibility in mind and should therefore try P—B4 now.

18. K—B1	**K—B3**
19. K—K2	**P—B5!**

From now on White will be reduced to complete passivity with his B little more than an ornament.

20. B—B3	**P—KN4**
21. P—KN4	**R—Q5**
22. P—KR3	

White has to place more and more pawns on white squares, so as to protect those that are already there.

22. ...,	**R—R1**
23. R x R	**P x R**
24. K—Q3	**K—K4**
25. B—K2	

If now 25. ..., P—KR4; 26. PxP, BxP; 27. R—KN1! But Black can prepare the advance of the RP systematically, i.e. without giving up material. Meanwhile, White's decision to use the R on the K-side has allowed Black access to the important square K4, but this is typical of such endings — as soon as you stop one gap another opens.

25. ...,	**B—B2**
26. R—KN1	**B—N3**
27. P—B3	**P—B4**
28. R—N1	**P—QR4**
29. P—QR4	

White locks the Queen-side and resigns himself to complete passivity in the hope that he will have sufficient tempo moves to guard against an entry of the black pieces by *zugzwang*. It almost works. From now to the time control Black plays about a little till just at adjournment time he has all his pieces in their ideal positions.

29. ...,	**P—R4**
30. R—N1	**K—B3**
31. R—Q1	**P x P**
32. RP x P	**K—K4**
33. R—K1	**R—R6**
34. B—Q1	

Guarding against BxPch.

34. ...,	**R—N6**
35. K—Q2	**R—R6**
36. K—Q3	**B—K1**
37. R—N1	**B—Q2**
38. K—Q2	

Black threatened 38. ..., R—N6; 39. R any, BxNP.

38. ...,	**B—K3**
39. R—N2	**R—R8**
40. B—B2	**R—R6**

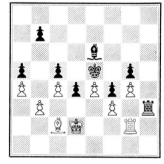

This is the critical position. White has to protect the BP, for which purpose three moves offer themselves:

(a) 41. B—Q1, R—N6!; 42. R—R2 (or 42. RxR, PxR; 43. K—K2, P—Q6ch; 44. K—B1, K—B5; 45. K—N2, K—K6; 46, KxP, K—Q7; etc.), P—Q6!; 43. R—R6 (or 43. KxP, BxNP), K—Q5; 44. RxB, R—N7ch; 45. K—B1, K—B6; and White has no defence against P—Q7ch.

(b) 41. R—B2, R—N6; 42. K—K2, BxNP!; 43. PxB, R—K6ch; 44. K—Q2, P—B6; 45. B—Q3, K—

B5; the KNP falls and the black K-side pawns win.

(c) the text.

41. K—K2 P—Q6 ch!

This was the sealed move.

42. B x P K—Q5

43. B—B2

Possibly overlooking Black's 45th move. "Relatively" best was 43. P—K5!, K—B6; 44. B—B5, R—R3; 45. R—N1, KxP; 46. R—N1ch, K—B6; 47. RxP, BxPch; 48. K—B2, R—R7ch; 49. K—N1, R—K7! Now the white KP is securely held and Black threatens both to bring the K over to KB6 for mate, and to advance the QBP. (50. B—K4 is refuted by B—Q6.)

43. ..., K—B6

44. B—Q1 R—R8

45. R—B2

This is what White has been playing for: the R move saves him from complete *zugzwang*. What can Black do now?

45. ..., P—N4!

The chess reporter of the London *Times* said to me afterwards: "Surely you didn't mean to play the P there. Lucky you happened to push it there with your elbow."

46. BP x P

46. RPxP, P—R5; loses at once.

46. ..., P—B5!

47. R—B1!

Clearly the pawn cannot be taken because the B would recapture with mate. But the text sets a clever trap: if Black — drunk with dreams of victory — pounces on the booty with 47. ..., RxR?; 48. KxR, PxP; 49. BxP!, KxB; 50. P—N6, B—B1; 51. P—K5, White actually wins, because the B cannot stop the parallel advance of the pawns; and if 47. ..., R—R1; 48. PxP, BxPch; 49. K—K1, the outcome is at least doubtful. But Black has an immediately fatal "zwischenzug":

47. ..., R—R7 ch!

48. R—B2 R—R1

Resigns.

For if now 49. PxP, BxPch; and mate in two; therefore White has to lose a piece without compensation.

Game No. 20.

As Yanofsky's second at the Interzonal tournament in Stockholm 1962 I tried to interest my principal in the "Alapin Sicilian" with which I had had quite a run of successes. However, he would not hear of it. It was Bisguier, staying in the same hotel, who showed an interest and eventually adopted the opening against Bobby Fischer. On that occasion I showed him the following game, which had been awarded the prize for the best-played game at the South African championship Durban 1957. Almost involuntarily he burst out with "But this is a very good game!" What he meant to say, of course, was "How could two patzers like you and Wolpert produce such a game?" It was the most sincere compliment I have ever had on any of my games.

Black: J. Wolpert.

Sicilian Defence.

1. P—K4 P—QB4

2. P—QB3 N—KB3

3. P—K5 N—Q4

4. N—B3 N—QB3

5. N—R3

Introduced by Canal against Van Scheltinga at Venice 1953, this move is probably the most flexible in this position. If at all possible, White will advance his QP only when he can recapture on his Q4 with pieces. My game against Larsen at Habana 1966 (see No. 44) shows how Black should react against this plan.

5. ..., P—QR3(?)

This, with the subsequent attack on

the KP, is too slow and involves Black in serious difficulties. In the game referred to in the introduction Fischer continued with 5. . . . , P—KN3; 6. P—KN3, B—N2; 7. B—N2, N—B2!; 8. Q—K2, O—O; 9. O—O, P—Q3. He obtained a slight initiative, but won the game only after Bisguier got too cocky.

	6. P—KN3	P—K3
	7. B—N2	Q—B2
	8. O—O!	

Demonstrating the harmlessness of Black's attack on the KP. If now 8. . . . , NxP?; 9. NxN, QxN; 10. R—K1, Q—B4; 11. B—K4, or 10. . . . , Q—Q3; 11. N—B4, Q—B3; 12. BxN, QxB; 13. N—N6.

	8. . . . ,	N—N3
	9. P—Q4	P x P
	10. P x P	

In the line chosen by Black White has no objection to recapturing with the pawn because the black Queen invites attacks on the open QB-file.

	10. . . . ,	B x N

So as to obtain a strongpoint on QB5, but the weakness of the black squares is a high price to pay.

	11. P x B	P—Q4
	12. Q—Q3	

Leading into the type of position with which White is familiar from his favourite variation of the Caro-Kann (compare game No. 26), which is characterized by the disappearance of Black's black-squared B, the doubling of the white QRP and Black's strongpoint on QB5. Here the circumstance that the white-squared Bishops are still on the board rather favours White. However, the gambit continuation, 12. PxP e.p., QxP; 13. B—B4, QxRP; 14. N—N5, might have been even better.

	12. . . . ,	B—Q2
	13. B—Q2	N—B5
	14. KR—B1	N x B?

Surrenders everything Black has been playing for. The point of the move is that Black wants to castle quickly but an immediate 14. . . . , O—O?; would allow 15. N—N5, P—KN3; 16. RxN!, PxR; 17. QxP, when the weakness of the black squares in the King's field is fatal. But 14. . . . , QR—B1!; would have made a much better fight of it, for if then 15. N—N5, P—R3; 16. N—K4, P—QN4! would force the white Knight to declare itself (17. N—B5?, as given by Euwe's Archives, is not playable because of 17. . . . , N(3)xKP!

	15. N x N	O—O
	16. N—N3	P—QN3
	17. R—B3	KR—B1
	18. R(1)—QB1	Q—N2

This turns out badly after White's 20th move, better defensive chances being offered by 18. . . . , Q—Q1.

	19. B—B1!	P—QR4

Otherwise the RP remains *en prise* when Black doubles Rooks on the QB-file. The alternative, 19. . . . , N—R4; suggested by Dreyer, is dealt with by 20. RxRch, RxR; 21. RxRch! (but not 21. QxP?, QxQ; 22. BxQ, NxN!; 23. BxR, NxR; 24 .BxB, N—K7ch; a variation discovered by Guy Miller), BxR; 22. NxN, PxN; 23. Q—QB3, P—R5; 24. Q—R5, Q—Q2; 25. B—Q3!, P—KB3 (best, as Kirby and I established in a lengthy correspondence); 26. B—B2, PxP; 27. BxP, Q—K2; 28. PxP. Now 28. . . . , B—N2? is immediately refuted by 29. Q—N6; if, however, 28. . . . , P—R3; 29. Q—N4, Q—QB2 (to get a somewhat nebulous perpetual check); 30. Q—Q6!, Q—B5; 31. Q—B6, QxQ; 32. BxQ, and the ending is won because the white King cannot ultimately be kept out of his Q4/QB5, e.g. 32. . . . , P—QR4; 33. P—QR4, B—R3; 34. B—N5, B—N2; 35. K—B1, P—Q5 (passive play is hopeless in this type of ending); 36. K—K2, B—K5; 37. B—Q3, B—B3 (or 37. . . . , B—N2; 38. B—B4!); 38. B—B2!, B—K1; 39.

51

B—N3 and wins. This slow ending is, of course, a far cry from the colourful happenings on the board.

20. Q—N1!

With the threat of 21. N—B5.

20. ...,   R—B2

Or 20. ..., QR—N1; 21. B—Q3, P—R3; 22. R(1)—B2, threatening both 23. Q—KB1, and 23. Q—QB1.

21. B—N5   QR—QB1

22. B x N   B x B!

Not 22. ..., RxB; 23. NxP!, RxR; 24. RxR, Q—R3; 25. RxRch, BxR; 26. N—B6! with a clearly won ending. With the text Black tries to inveigle White into a similar simplification, but after 23. NxP?, PxN; 24. QxQ, RxQ; 25. RxB, RxR; 26. RxR, P—N3; Black threatens to attack the QP from the rear (27. R—R6, R—N8ch; 28. K—N2, R—Q8).

23. Q—B2!

Resisting the temptation and bringing about a position reminiscent of the famous game, Alekhine - Niemzovich, San Remo 1930. Exactly as in that game Black now tries to play his King to the other side so as to relieve the deadly immobilisation of his pieces. White threatened 24. P—QR4, followed by N—Q2—N1—R3—N5, and 23. ..., P—R5; would not help because of 23. N—Q2—B3—K1—Q3—N4.

23. ...,   P—N3

24. N—Q2   K—B1

25. N—B3   K—K1

Played in extreme time pressure, this move allows the quiet positional game to end in a blaze of glory. How-

ever, against the leisurely rambling of the Knight nothing would have helped, e.g., 25. ..., P—R3; 26. N—R4, P—KN4; 27. N—N2, K—K1; 28. N—K3, K—Q1; 29. N—N4, P—R4; 30. N—B6, followed by 31. Q—R7. Or the more amusing 26, ..., K—K2; 27. NxNPch!, PxN; 28. QxP, B—K1 (if 28. ..., R—B1; 29. QxRP, and the KRP marches through); 29. Q—B6ch, K—Q2; 30. Q—B8! If now 30. ..., R—B3; 31. Q—N7ch, wins the Queen, and otherwise the threat of Q—Q6ch (at present mate) is fatal. In this variation the lone white Queen paralyses the whole black army.

26. N—N5   P—R3

27. N x KP!

27. ...,	P x N
28. Q x P ch	K—K2
29. Q—B6 ch	K—Q2
30. Q—B7 ch	K—Q1
31. Q—B8 ch	B—K1
32. Q—Q6 ch	B—Q2
33. R—B3!	

The final thunderbolt. After 33. ..., RxRch; 34. K—N2, Black cannot stop the mate on B8. He therefore resigned.

Game No. 21.

Played in the South African championship Durban 1957, the following game shows the *strength* of the "bad" Bishop — i.e. the Bishop of the colour of the squares on which most of your own pawns are permanently placed. What is only too often overlooked by near-experts is the fact that strategically-placed pawns also confine the opponent's Bishop to narrow quarters ("he bites on granite") and at the same time lend support to their own Bishop IF there is an avenue by which he can enter the opponent's game. A famous contemporary example is the fine game Yanofsky won from Uhlmann at the Stockholm Interzonal of 1962, which was won almost single-handed by the allegedly bad Bishop.

Black: K. V. Grivainis.
Centre Counter Defence.

1. P—K4	P—Q4
2. P x P	N—KB3
3. B—N5 ch	

Retaining the pawn for a few moves and thus forcing Black into a narrow path of development in order to regain it.

3. . . . ,	B—Q2
4. B—B4	B—N5
5. P—KB3	B—B4
6. N—B3	QN—Q2
7. KN—K2	N—N3
8. P—Q3	KN x P
9. N x N	N x N
10. N—N3	B—N3
11. P—B4	P—K3

"As a result of his backward development and the paralysis of his QB, the black position already carries the germ of death in it," Tartakower, in his usual picturesque and somewhat exaggerating style, commented on the identical opening moves of the game Maroczy - Miss Menchik, Carlsbad 1929.

12. Q—B3	P—QB3
13. O—O	B—B4 ch

To be considered is 13. . . . , N—K2; with P—KR4 and N—B4 to follow, for the Bishop is not happily placed on its present diagonal.

14. K—R1	N—K2
15. N—K4	B—N3
16. P—B3	N—B4
17. N—N5	Q—K2
18. P—QR4	

Loosening up the Q-side and preparing for B—QR3.

18. . . . ,	P—QR4
19. P—QN3	N—Q3
20. B—R3	Q—Q2
21. P—Q4!	

The KB is expendable: its capture strengthens White's centre and opens the N-file, which will play an important role throughout the game. The sacrificial assault 21. NxKP?, PxN; 22. BxP, QxB; 23. QR—K1, K—Q2; 24. RxQ, KxR; does not yield enough, Black keeping Rook and two minor pieces for the Queen. But Black has to be on his guard. . . .

21. . . . ,	N x B

Which is why he refrains from the move one would expect at this stage (when the N cannot go to K4): 21. . . . , P—KR3. In that case White could really play 22. NxKP!, PxN; 23. BxP, QxB; 24. QR—K1. If then 24. . . . , K—Q2; 25. RxQ, KxR; 26. R—K1ch, K—Q2; 27. Q—N4ch, B—B4; 28. QxPch, and wins, the fact that the QB has lost its protection making all the difference vis-a-vis the previous note. And if 24. . . . , B—K5 (24. . . . , N—K5 ; 25. P—B5, would return *both* pieces); 25. P—B5! If Black takes the pawn, no matter how, he will again lose both pieces, so he has to choose between 25. . . . , BxQ; 26. RxQch, K—B2; 27. RxN, and White wins at least a third pawn with a very strong position; or 25. . . . , Q—K2; 26. BxN, QxB; 27. RxBch, K any; 28. R—K6, and it is doubtful whether the black King can survive (28. . . . , Q—Q4?; is not playable because of 29.

QxQ, exploiting the miserable position of the black B). Thus there was a great deal of thought behind the exchange in the text.

22.	P x N	B—Q1
23.	N—K4	B—K2
24.	KR—N1	O—O
25.	R—N6	Q—B2
26.	P—B5!	B x N
27.	Q x B	

At this stage Black was quite happy — by superficial standards he has the "good", his opponent the "bad" bishop. Actually his Bishop has no scope at all whereas White's will — by a long slow journey — be brought to a very powerful post.

27.	...,	KR—Q1
28.	QR—N1	QR—N1
29.	K—N1!	

White wants to play his B back to B1, but cannot do so at once because of the reply, BxP! So the mate on the back rank must be guarded first.

29.	...,	B—B3
30.	B—B1	P—N3
31.	B—K3	R—Q2
32.	B—B2	

Ready to go to N3 and exploit the fatal weakness of the diagonal at the end of which the defenders of the QNP have their gathering. The black B is powerless to do anything about it. He now makes a last attempt to use his pawns for stopping the occupation of the deadly diagonal.

32.	...,	P—R4
33.	P—KR3	K—N2
34.	P—N4	P x P
35.	P x P	R—KR1
36.	P—N5	B x NP

With three seconds left on his clock for the last move before time is up, Black produces this flash of genius. If now 37. PxB, Q—R7ch; 38. K—B1, R—Q4! Black would conjure up most promising complications. But with the B *en prise*, White can afford to execute his latent threat on the QN-file.

37. R x NP!   **Resigns**

Naturally, if Black had played the modest 36. ..., B—K2; White would not have chosen this transaction but continued 37. B—N3, with systematic suffocation.

Game No. 22.

Where is the chess player who does not wish to make a good impression on entering a new sphere of activity? Thus I could be well satisfied that my first tournament game on taking up residence in Dublin, played in the Dublin League 1957, was afterwards awarded the *Irish Times* prize for the best game of the year. My opponent was a young player who had played as a reserve for Ireland at the Moscow team tournament where, after a shaky start, he had finished with a creditable +1 =4 −0 in the finals.

White: R. Grogan.
French Defence.

1.	P—K4	P—K3
2.	P—Q4	P—Q4
3.	N—Q2	N—KB3
4.	P—K5	KN—Q2
5.	B—Q3	

The modern line with 5. P—KB4, P—QB4; 6. P—B3, N—QB3; 7. QN—B3, Q—N3; 8. P—KN3, PxP; 9. PxP, B—N5ch; 10. K—B2 (introduced

by Portisch against Tal at Oberhausen 1961), seems to make it harder for Black to get a fully satisfactory game.

5.	...,	P—QB4
6.	P—QB3	N—QB3
7.	N—K2	P x P

Now regarded as the best method of assaulting the White centre. In the two Italian tournaments at San Benedetto and Ancona 1956 I had adways adopted Lothar Schmid's favourite line, 7. ..., Q—N3; 8. N—B3, PxP; 9. PxP, P—B3; but though I succeeded in scoring 3½ points out of five games with this line, I ended up doubting its merit — and this seems to be the consensus of opinion today.

8. P x P   P—B3
9. P x P

Avoiding the dubious complications of the N excursion to KB4 (as e.g. in the game Niephaus-Stahlberg, Wageningen 1957, which was played just prior to the present game) in favour of a quieter line, but this does not mean that it is better.

9. ...,   Q x P
10. N—KB3   B—N5 ch
11. N—B3

Now White has taken two moves for each Knight to reach their natural squares KB3 and QB3. As a result Black is ahead in development and could immediately resolve the tension in the centre by 11. ..., P—K4 (as in Milic-Czerniak, Belgrade 1955). However, he prefers a fuller game for the time being.

11. ...,   O—O
12. O—O   P—KR3
13. B—B2   R—B2

So as to have N—B1 in case of need. Temporarily Black's pieces are in each other's way, which induces White to overplay his hand.

14. P—KR4?

Even though the QP has to be given up in the process, the advance P—K4 is now very strong — largely as a result of the weakening of the white K position.

14. ...,   B x N
15. P x B   P—K4!
16. P x P   N(2) x P
17. N x N

This fails to a simple *zwischenzug*. More dangerous was the immediate 17. QxP, NxNch; 18. PxN. Now Black must not play 18. ..., QxKBP; because the cunning 19. B—N3! — another *zwischenzug* — would win the exchange. Black in his turn might resort to a *zwischenzug*, 18. ..., B—R6; when 19. B—N3, is not playable because of 19. ..., Q—N3ch; with mate to follow, and 19. R—K1 would now allow 19. ..., QxKBP. But after 19. Q—K4!, BxR; 20. Q—R7ch, K—B1; 21. B—R3ch, K—K1; 22. Q—N 8ch, the chances are very unclear, and Black need not let himself in for such a wild scramble. He has the solid move, 18. ..., B—K3!; and if then 19. Q—K4, P—KN3!; threatening 20. ..., B—B4; while the NP itself is protected by the pin on the N-file. This seems to work out in Black's favour in all variations.

17. ...,   Q x N
18. R—K1   B—N5!
19. Q—Q2   Q—R4
20. Q—Q3   R—B3!

The check on R7 is now quite innocuous and would merely displace the white Q. Black's position is so strong that he need not allow any exchanges. White's main weakness, the KRP, cannot be protected by P—N3 because the black Knight would enter via K4 and B6.

21. B—K3   R—Q1
22. QR—N1   B—B4
23. Q—K2   Q x P
24. B x B   R x B

25. R x P **R—R4**
26. P—KB4

Here my opponent's flag was trembling on the brink, and it was obvious that anything in the slightest unexpected would push him over. I therefore played:

26. ..., **N—K4!**

and he promptly exceeded the time limit. The game was always lost, for if 27. PxN?, Q—R7ch; 28. K—B2, R—B4ch; 29. B—B4, RxBch; 30. K—K3, R—K5ch, etc.

Or 27. B—Q4? (so as to *win* after 27. ..., N—N5?; 28. RxPch), N—B6ch; 28. PxN, Q—N6ch; 29. Q—N2, QxRch; 30. Q—B1, R—R8ch; or 27. RxPch?, KxR; 28. B—Q4, Q—R7ch, followed by 29. ..., QxBPch. "Relatively" best was 27. QxR!, QxQ; 28. PxN, QxP; 29. B—B2, QxP; 30. R(1)—K7, Q—B3. If now 31. B—N3 (so as to threaten B—K5), Black plays 31. ..., R—QB1! and wins (31. B—K5, R—B8ch; 32. K—R2, Q—R5 mate). -

Game No. 23.

The following game from the Greece-South Africa match at the Munich Olympiad 1958 is one of the most interesting I have ever played — thanks largely to the ingenious play, in both middle and end-game, of my young opponent. My own contribution is the far more modest one of an unusual opening (for which see also my game against Fricker, No. 16).

Black: T. Angos.
French Defence, Alapin Gambit.

1. P—K4 **P—K3**
2. P—Q4 **P—Q4**
3. B—K3 **P x P**
4. P—KB3 **N—KB3**
5. P x P **P—K4**

A new idea. At this point White cannot play 6. PxP, because after the exchange of Queens N—N5 would be unpleasant. On the other hand, to waste a move (P—K3—K4) in so open a position can hardly be correct.

6. N—KB3 **B—KN5**
7. B—N5 ch

So as to close square QB6 to the black Knight after B—B4.

7. ..., **P—B3**
8. B—QB4 **B x N**
9. Q x B?

Much too carefree. Black having refused the gambit pawn, there is no need to insist on making the game a gambit. After 9. PxB! White has two Bishops, the better centre and the open KN-file at virtually no positional cost.

9. ..., **P x P**
10. B—KN5 **Q—R4 ch**
11. B—Q2 **Q—QB4**

If 11. ..., Q—N3; 12. P—K5!, offering the QR. Now White regains his pawn, but not for long.

12. Q—QN3 **QN—Q2**
13. B x P ch **K—Q1**
14. N—R3?!

Suddenly White realises that he, rather than the opponent, is in danger of falling behind in development. He therefore re-invests the pawn to take the initiative again — and if anybody should have unkind remarks to make about the opening play in this game, I am in full agreement with him.

14. ..., **N x P**
15. O—O—O **N x B**
16. R x N **B—K2**
17. K—N1 **B—N4**

So as to force the R off the Q-file before White has time to double Rooks and play P—B3.

18. R—K2 **R—KB1?**

To stop the N from reaching B4

and also to drive the B to unfavourable squares. However, the first objective could have been obtained more rationally by 18. ..., P—QN4! — and as regards the second, the B commands one very powerful square indeed.

19. B—K6!

Threatening both BxN and QxP, while the seemingly forced reply 19. ..., N—N3; would allow 20. Q—N3 (threat R—K5), B—B3; 21. P—B3. Is Black lost?

19. ...,	P—QN4!
20. B x N	K x B
21. Q—K6 ch	K—B2!

And not the "cautious" 21. ..., K—Q1?; 22. R—K5, Q—K2; 23. QxP and wins. With the text Black relies on a beautiful and unusual defensive combination.

22. R—K5   Q—N5!!

This move does not exhaust itself in the obvious mate on K8, which is merely a motif in the plan: the surprising idea to exchange Queens when a piece down! For if now 23. RxB, QR—K1; 24. RxPch, K—N3; 25. P—B3, RxQ! (better than exchanging Queens after 25. ..., PxP; 26. Q—N3); 26. PxQ, R—B7; with the unanswerable threat of doubling Rooks on the 7th rank. If e.g. 27. R—QB1?, R(3)—K7; 28. R—B2, P—Q6!; 29. RxR, R—B8ch; and mate next move. White would have nothing better than 27. R—N3, R(3)—K7; 28. R—N3,

when he would be tied hand and foot with no method of disentangling himself.

23. N x P ch!

Therefore White relinquishes the win of a piece.

23. ...,	P x N
24. P—QR3?	

Afterwards it is easy to say that 24. RxB, QR—K1; 25. RxPch, K—N1; 26. P—QR3, QxPch; 27. KxQ, RxQ; 28. R—Q1! offered better winning chances because of the disconnected black pawns and the bad position of his King. With an ending two pawns up White felt quite satisfied, but he has none of the positional trumps mentioned above.

24. ...,	Q—B5

Not 24. ..., Q—Q7?; 25. R—B5ch, with mate to follow. After the text White has to exchange Queens, for 25. Q—R6, is refuted by 25. ..., P—Q6.

25. Q x Q	P x Q
26. R x B	K—B3

Not 26. ..., K—Q3?; 27. R—Q1, and wins.

27. R—Q1	QR—Q1
28. R x NP	R—B7
29. R x KRP	P—Q6!
30. P x P	R—QN1

Still simpler was 30. ..., P—B6!; 31. R—QB1, RxPch; 32. K—R1, R—N6; 33. RxP, RxQP; 34. R—R8 (so as to tie both Rooks to the defence of the pawn), K—N2!; 35. R—R4, R—Q7; 36. R—N4ch, RxR; 37. PxR, RxP; and draws. But the text also forces the draw, though Black still has to watch out for some traps.

31. P—QN4	P x P e.p.
32. P—Q4	R—K1
33. R—R3	

By playing 33. P—Q5ch immediately, White could gain a move compared with the same idea a move later, but if the black K stays in front of the pawn it would make no difference to the outcome.

33. ...,	**R x P**
34. P—Q5 ch	**K—Q3**
35. R—R6 ch	**K—Q2!**

And not 35. ..., K—B4; 36. R—B
6ch, K—N4; 37. R(1)—QB1!, P—N7;
38. R(1)—B5ch, K—R5; 39. K—R2
(threatening mate, and if in reply, 39.
..., P—R4?; 40. R—B4ch, K—N4;

41. P—R4 mate!), P—N8(Q) dbl ch;
40. KxQ, and White retains winning
chances.

36. R—R3	**R(1)—K7**
37. R x P	**R x P**
38. P—Q6	**R—Q7**
39. R—N7 ch	**K x P**

Draw agreed.

Game No. 24.

It is by no means co-incidental that of the five games against German players
I have included in this volume from my period in Frankfurt/Main, no fewer
than three were played in matches between my club, *Königsspringer*, and their
traditional rivals, *Schachfreunde*. There was such bitter competition, and at
times even bad blood, between these two clubs that each member of each team
tried to give his best on each occasion. The following game was the first of
these encounters, played early in 1959 shortly after my joining the club; the
other two are those against Peters (No. 27) and Dr. Palme (No. 35).

White: M. Graefe.
French Defence.

1. P—K4	**P—K3**
2. P—Q4	**P—Q4**
3. P—K5	**P—QB4**
4. P—QB3	**Q—N3**

Wade's idea: the development of the
QN is held back in order to exchange
Black's "problem child", the QB. An
interesting modern attempt at crossing
Black's plan is 5. B—Q3, B—Q2; 6.
PxP?!, BxP; 7. Q—K2.

5. N—B3	**B—Q2**
6. P—QR3	

This plays into Black's hands —
what Black wants is a queenless ending
to be "won" on the white squares.
Naturally this is a long way off.

6. ...,	**B—N4**
7. B x B	**Q x B**
8. Q—K2	**Q x Q ch**
9. K x Q	**N—QB3**
10. B—K3	**P x P**
11. P x P	**KN—K2**
12. N—B3	**N—B1!**

Black wants to play his other N to
QR4 and this one via QN3 to QB5 —
at the same time the N helps to hold

square Q3 for the time being (see
following note).

13. N—QR4

Stopping an immediate 13. ...,
N—N3. Against the interesting idea,
13. N—QN5, K—Q2; 14. N—N5,
Black may have to fall back on the
modest 14. ..., P—QR3!; 15. NxBP,
R—KN1; 16. N(5)—Q6, NxN; 17.
PxN, BxP; 18. NxB, KxN; for neither
of the complicated exchange sacrifice
variations seems to be quite correct:
(a) 14. ..., P—B3; 15. NxKP!, KxN;
16. N—B7ch, K—Q2; 17. NxR, or
(b) 14. ..., P—QR3; 15. NxBP, PxN?!;
16. NxR, K—K1; 17. P—KR4! Either
N can be extricated in time.

13. ...,	**P—B3**
14. P—R4	**P—QN4!**
15. QR—B1	

Ensuring that the N reaches QB5
after all (it could not go there at once
because the KP hangs), but the bold
horseman will be in constant jeopardy
on that square despite the imaginative
relief action on the other wing.

15. ...,	**N—R4**
16. N—B5	**K—B2**

17. P—KN4

It looks as though the advance P—KN5 will throw the black game into disorder, but Black's break in the centre comes first.

17. ...,	N—N3
18. P—N5	N(N)—B5!
19. NP x P	P x P
20. P x P	B x N
21. P x B	P—K4!

This is the point of the black action: the white B is kept off the long diagonal — the recapture of the pawn can wait.

22. N—Q2?!

It is difficult to assess White's most promising plan in this position. With the text he plays for the removal of the black N from the commanding position on QB5 (though this is purely temporary) and the re-opening of the long black diagonal by P—KB4. He will then play for mate (based on the strength of the KBP) — but so will Black!

| 22. ..., | N x NP |
| 23. P—B4! | |

If 23. R—QN1, Black keeps his booty by 23. ..., N—R5.

| 23. ..., | P x P |
| 24. B—Q4 | |

Now it is White who is a pawn down, but his pieces seem to co-operate beautifully, the black K is endangered and the black pieces dispersed in all directions. However, the following check turns the tables again:

square K5 becomes the pivot of Black's counter-play.

24. ...,	KR—K1 ch!
25. K—B3	N(N)—B5
26. N x N	N x N
27. KR—N1	N—Q7 ch
28. K x P	R—K5 ch
29. K—B5	N—B6!

Of course not 29. ..., RxB?; 30. R—N7ch, K—B1; 31. R(1)—KN1.

30. R—N7 ch	K—B1
31. B—B2	QR—K1
32. R—K7(?)	

White has to find a defence against the threat of R(1)—K4 mate, but the text leads to a hopeless ending. The best try was the bold 32. RxKRP!, when the black King is still not out of trouble and the two white BP's are threatening. Black would have to play very accurately, thus: 32. ..., R(1)—K4ch; 33. K—N6, R—N5ch; 34. K—R6, R—B4! (best — neither 34. ..., R—K7; nor 34. ..., NxP; cope with the threat of the QBP); 35. P—B6, RxPch; 36. K—R5, N—K4! (threatening mate by 37. ..., R—B4ch; and 38. ..., R—N3); 37. R—KN1, R—B4 ch; 38. K—R6, RxB; 39. RxR (or 39. P—B7, RxPch; 40. K—N5, R—QB5; 41. P—B8(Q)ch, RxQ; 42. R—R8ch, K—N2; 43. RxR, N—B6ch; and wins), NxRch; 40. K—N5, N—B3!; and Black tames the QBP. The rest is easy.

32. ...,	R(1) x R
33. P x R ch	K x P
34. R—Q1	N x P ch
35. B x N	R x B
36. K—N5	R—QR5
37. R x P	R x P
38. P—B6	P—QR3
39. R—Q7 ch	K—K3
40. R x P	K—Q3
41. P—B7	R—QB6
42. R—R6 ch	K—Q4
43. R—R7	R—B3
44. K—B4	P—N5

45. K—K3	K—B5
46. R—R1	K—N4
47. R—R7	K—N3
Resigns.	

A game of unusual complexion —
with both sides playing so sharply for
their (Queenless) mating attacks, it is
perhaps not surprising that from the
12th to about the 30th move my
opponent thought he was winning.

Game No. 25.

The old rule that if you wish to mount a king-side attack, you have to be
safe in the centre can be disregarded only in exceptional circumstances. In this
game from the South African championship at Johannesburg 1959 — at a time
when I held both the South African and Irish titles but was domiciled in
Germany! — White thus fights for a positionally lost cause after his 10th move,
but this does not mean that in practice his attack could not become very
dangerous.

White: D. Lewis.
French Defence.

1. P—K4	P—K3
2. P—Q4	P—Q4
3. N—QB3	N—KB3
4. B—N5	B—K2
5. B x N	

The Anderssen Attack, a harmless
line which Lewis may have adopted
because in former years I used to be
partial to the inferior defence, 5. ...,
BxB; 6. P—K5, B—K2; 7. Q—N4,
P—KN3(?). After 7. ..., O—O; as in
the game, Black need not fear the
white attack as long as he quickly
opens lines against White's own King
— if necessary, at the expense of a
pawn.

5. ...,	B x B
6. P—K5	B—K2
7. Q—N4	O—O
8. O—O—O	P—QB4
9. P x P	N—B3
10. N—B3?	

This is the error referred to in the
introduction. The white game stands
and falls by the rapidity with which
he can mount a King-side attack, but
to do so his pivotal K5-square must
be secure. 10. P—B4, was thus necessary. (For a similar attack, without
P—KB4, but under greater provoca-
tion, see game No. 45 — even in the
somewhat exceptional circumstances

of that opening White had to worry
about his loose pawn centre.)

10. ...,	P—B4
11. Q—N3	

He is already uneasy about the inadequate support of K5 — normal is
11. Q—R3, with the idea of an early
P—KN4.

11. ...,	B x P
72. P—KR4	

A poor substitute for the normal
attack in this variation.

12. .-.,	Q—R4
13. K—N1	B—Q2
14. P—R5	P—QN4

The accepted procedure against the
P—KN4 attack, which may not be
necessary in the changed circumstances. It is clear that after the
obvious 15. BxP, QR—N1; the black
attack would be quicker than the
white one, but White now skilfully
combines the threat of a deferred
capture with designs against KN6.

15. P—R6	P—N3
16. N—KR4	P—B5!

Black is prepared. With this move
he starts on a series of *petites com-
binaisons* designed to thwart the
threats White develops.

17. Q—R3	N x P
18. B x P!	

Now possible, for if 18. ..., BxB?;
19. QxPch, N—B2; 20. NxNP, KR—

60

K1; 21. Q—KB6, NxP; 22. Q—R8ch, and wins. In fact, the threat of 19. BxB, is most unpleasant. Has Black overplayed his hand?

18. ...,   **B—B1!**

This quiet retreat maintains Black's attack.

19. KR—K1   **N—B2**
20. Q—Q3   **N x P**
21. N x NP!

Not 21. NxQP?, PxN; 22. QxQPch, N—B2; 23. QxB, P—QR3; 24. Q—Q5, PxB.

21. ...,   **R—B3**
22. N—K5   **B x P**
23. R—KB1

If now 23. NxP, PxN; 24. QxQPch, B—K3; 25. QxRch, R—B1; 26. Q—B6!, QxPch; 27. K—B1, BxR; 28. RxB, R—Q1!; 29. Q—R6, Q—Q4; and if now 30. QxBch, QxQ; 31. B—B4, R—Q4! (32. N—Q3, Q—QB3; 33. N—K5, Q—B4) and wins.

23. ...,   **B—K6**

24. N x P?

At last White falls for the bait Black has been dangling before his eyes all the time, whereupon his game collapses at once. That, however, the black attack is more dangerous is illustrated by the wild variation, 24. P—KN3, P—R3!; 25. PxP, PxB; 26. QxB, P—N5; 27. R—N1ch, K—B1; 28. Q—N3, PxN; 29. Q—N7ch, K—K1; and the momentary standstill of the white assault suffices to lose the game for him. If, in this line, White chooses the quieter 25. B—B6, R—R2!; 26. PxP, BxP; 27. R—N1ch, R—N2; 28. RxRch, KxR; 29. R—N1ch, K—R1; he will have no compensation for the pawn minus and Black's strong centre.

24. ...,   **P x N**
25. Q x P ch   **B—K3**
26. Q x R ch   **R—B1**
27. N—B4

This looks like a way out because White could recapture on B4 with a check, but it is only a delusion.

27. ...,   **Q x B**
28. R—Q8   **Q x N!**
29. R x R ch   **K—N2**
Resigns.

Black threatens both QxR mate and QxRP mate, and there is no useful check.

Game No. 26.

Played at the Valentin Marin Memorial (Zonal) tournament Madrid 1960, the following game pleased both contestants so much that they entered it jointly for the best game award. Though unsuccessful in this quest, I believed that, apart from Black's inaccuracy on move 15, both sides made the most of their chances — until a re-examination on preparing the present volume has raised doubts in my mind.

Black: L. Pachman.
Caro-Kann Defence.

1. P—K4	P—QB3		5. N—N3	B—N3
2. P—Q4	P—Q4		6. P—KR4	P—KR3
3. P—K5	B—B4		7. P—R5	B—R2
4. N—K2	P—K3		8. P—QB3	

For an assessment of this opening (including the fact that there is no

61

objective need for the finesse in the text), see game No. 4.

8. ...,	P—QB4
9. B—Q3	B x B
10. Q x B	Q—N3
11. O—O	N—QB3
12. R—Q1	R—B1
13. N—R3	P x P
14. P x P	B x N
15. P x B	N—R4?

The doubling of White's QRP (depriving him of the possibility of P—QN3) and the resultant strong-point for the black Knight are reminiscent of Wolpert's play in game No. 20. But the weakening of the black squares is a high price to pay for these advantages. At least Black should now first look after his King-side and play 15. ..., KN—K2!; as Golombek did against me at the An Tostal tournament Dublin 1956.

16. R—N1	Q—B3
17. B—Q2	N—B5
18. P—B4	N—K2

The last chance of getting this N into play. At the Irish Championship Dublin 1969 Reilly tried to safeguard his Q-side pawns by 18. ..., P—QN3?; but after 19. P—B5, was reduced to 19. ..., NxB; 20. RxN, Q—B5; 21. PxP, QxQ; 22. PxPch, KxP; 23. RxQ, K—K3; 24. N—K2, with an ending that soon proved hopeless. The trouble is that after 19. ..., N—K2; 20. P—B6! the black Knight would have no decent square.

| 19. B—N4 | Q—Q2! |

Essential. In Heidenfeld - Pines, Johannesburg 1955, the Rhodesian champion tried 19. ..., P—R4 immediately, but after 20. BxN, KxB; 21. P—B5, R—B2; 22. R—KB1, Q—K1; 23. R—B2, K—Q1; 24. N—K2! found that his pieces had got into a helpless tangle.

20. P—B5!

Now much stronger than 20. BxN?, QxB; 21. P—B5, O—O!; 22. R—KB1,

QxP; 23. R—N3, QxP!; with strong counter-threats.

20. ...,	KN x P
21. N x N	P x N
22. R—KB1	

Preparing to give up a piece.

| 22. ..., | P—R4 |
| 23. B—B5 | R—B3 |

Safeguarding the third rank and threatening to win the B. Has the white attack been refuted?

24. R x BP

| 24. ..., | P—QN3 |

Going for the win of the piece. Today it seems to me that 24. ..., N—Q7!; would have involved Black in less trouble, though this was by no means easy to judge in the game. If then 25. R—Q1, N—K5; 26. R(1)—KB1, NxB; 27. PxN, O—O; White's seemingly strong attacking position along the KB-file seems to yield nothing and his own pawn weaknesses may come to tell against him. Better would be 25. QxN!, QxR; 26. RxP! (not 26. R—KB1, Q—K3; 27. QxQRP, P—QN3!), RxB; 28. PxR, QxKP; when the white BP looks strong but his own King is exposed (e.g. 28. P—B6, O—O; 29. R—Q7, R—B1; 30. RxQP, Q—R8ch; 31. K—R2, RxP!).

| 25. QR—KB1! | P x B |
| 26. R x P | Q x R! |

Pachman saw only at the last moment that the surrender of the Queen for two Rooks, involving as it does the return of the extra piece as well, is forced. He intended 26. ..., Q—N5?; which is refuted by 27. R(1)—B4, QxRP (27. ..., Q—N4?; 28. Q—R3!, N—N3; 29. PxP and Black can no longer guard both Q2 and K3); 28. Q—QN3!, N—N3 (or 28. ..., R—N3; 29. Q—R4ch, while if 28. ..., QxR; 29. RxQ, KxR; 30. Q—N7ch); 29. PxP, RxP; 30. P—K6! with unanswerable threats. Faulty, however, would have been my intention, 26. ..., Q—N5; 27. R(1)—B4, QxRP; 28. RxP, R—KB1?; 29. RxRch, KxR; 30. Q—R7, Q—Q8ch; 31. K—R2, Q—R4ch; 32. K—N3, and wins, for Black would have played the sangfroid 28. ..., PxP!; and if then 29. Q—QN3, neither 29. ..., R—N3?; nor 29. ..., N—N3?; but 29. ..., QxKP!; 30. Q—N7, Q—K3!; and the white attack is held.

| 27. R x Q | K x R |
| 28. Q—B3 ch | K—K2 |

Clearly 28. ..., K—K3? would lose either R after 29. Q—N4ch.

29. Q x P	R(1)—QB1!
30. Q x N	P x P
31. Q x P	K—K3!
32. Q—N4 ch	

I could not see any progress after, say, 32. K—R2, R(1)—B2; so grabbed the NP while the grabbing was good.

32. ...,	K x P
33. Q x P ch	K—B4
34. K—R2	R(1)—B2
35. Q—Q4	K—K3

Draw agreed.

White cannot prevent the opponent from ultimately doubling R's on the third rank and keeping the K on the first or second (taking care only that the Rooks are not pinned). Black can then safely give up his QRP, as long as the KRP is protected. White's only winning attempt would then consist of establishing a passed pawn on the K-side; as soon, however, as this pawn tries to cross the sixth rank, Black gives up his 2 R's for Q + P, leaving White only with the useless doubled QRP. Thus at the very end the doubling of this P has shown a profit.

A few months later history repeated itself: at the Leipzig team tournament Tal used this identical Rook barrier on the third rank to draw his exciting game with Robatsch.

Game No. 27.

Played in the course of the Frankfurt league matches 1960, the following game is probably the most original I have ever played. By move 19, all Black's pieces — except one horseman stranded on a remote square in enemy territory — are assembled on the 1st and 2nd ranks, yet Black is in full control of the board.

White: M. Peters.
Dutch Defence (in effect).

1. P—QB4	P—KB4
2. N—QB3	N—KB3
3. P—KN3	P—K4
4. B—N2	P—Q3
5. P—Q4	B—K2

Now it is a normal Dutch set-up in which Black has been permitted to play P—K4 without a struggle — a pleasant debut from his point of view.

6. N—R3	O—O
7. O—O	Q—K1
8. P—B3	P x P(!)

Niemzovich would have called this move a sacrifice — of Black's square KB5 (on the whole it is a good deal easier to sacrifice squares than material). Black reasons that on the one hand his QB4 (see his 11th move) will be more useful to him than KB4 to his opponent and, on the other, White won't have the choice between P—Q5 and PxKP whenever it suits him to

63

play either.

9. N—QN5	**B—Q1**
10. N x P(Q4)	**N—B3**
11. N—QN5	

This N loses a great deal of time, enabling Black to build up a blockade on the Q-side. The threat of 11. ...., NxN; 12. QxN, QxP; could have been met by e.g. 11. N—B4.

11. ...,	**P—QR4**
12. B—Q2	**B—Q2!**

With the threat of 13. ..., N—K4; attacking both the QBP and the QN. But the cure adopted by White is worse than the disease: after R—B1 he is more or less committed to P—QR3, which leaves incurable weaknesses on the white squares.

13. R—B1	**QN—N5**
14. P—R3	**N—R3**
15. N—B3	**P—R5**
16. N—B4	**N—B4**
17. B—K1	**N—N6**
18. R—QB2	**Q—B2**
19. N(3)—Q5	**N—K1!**

The key-move to Black's conduct of the game. He now stands ready to dislodge both white Knights from their central positions, after which the housing shortage in the white camp becomes acute. In such positions the first consideration is to deny the opponent any chance to exchange pieces.

20. B—B2

20. P—K4, P—B3! would produce K-side square weaknesses in addition to those on the Q-side whether White replies 21. N—K3, B—N4; or 21. N—N4, P—KN4; 22. N—Q3, P—B5.

20. ...,	**P—KN4**
21. N—Q3	**B—K3**
22. P—B4	

Again, the alternative 22. P—K4 is inferior because of 22. ..., P—B5!; and if then 23. PxP, P—B3; 24. N—K3, PxP; 25. N—KN4, K—R1!; with the threat of 26. ...., P—R4. With the text White creates a variety of tactical chances because of the opening of the

diagonal of his white-squared B.

22. ...,	**P—B3**
23. N—K3	**P—N5**
24. P—B5?!	

A clever attempt at breaking the blockade — if necessary at the cost of material. For if now 24. ..., P—Q4; 25. N—K5, Q—K2; 26. P—R3! Then 26. ..., P—R4; is not playable because of 27. N—N6, and if 26. ..., NxP; 27. RxN!, QxR; 28. NxBP! and White gets excellent play for his pieces at trifling cost. Again, 26. ..., P—Q5; would not help because of 27. N(3)—B4, PxP; 28. BxRP, QxP; 29. P—K3!, PxP; 30. BxKP, Q—Q4; 31. Q—R5, N—B3; 32. Q—R6, and again White has enormous play. Finally, Black might answer 25. N—K5, with 25. ..., Q—N2; 26. P—R3, P—R4; 27. PxP, RPxP; when White would get dangerous chances after the piece sacrifice 28. NxQP?!, PxN; 29. BxP.

The attempt to get rid of the blockading black N by 24. N—B1?, on the other hand, is refuted by the amusing counter 24. ..., N—R8! when White loses material without benefit.

24. ..., **N—Q5!**

Avoiding all these speculative freing lines and getting his pieces into commanding positions instead.

25. R—B1	**B—N6**
26. Q—Q2	**B—R4**
27. N—N4	**P x P!**
28. R x P	**R—Q1**

And suddenly, as the result of one

open file, the board explodes. Black's obvious threat is 28. ..., N—B6ch; but the "win of the Queen" has to be treated with care after 29. QxN?(!), RxQ; 30. NxBP, when only the immediate return of the Queen by 30. ..., QxN!; 31. RxQ, RxR; 32. BxR, P—B4; with the win of a piece, secures the advantage — on any other reply White would actually win. The other way of surrendering the Queen, viz., 29. RxB, N—B6ch; 30. PxN, RxQ; 31. NxBP, Q—B3!; does not give White enough.

29. B—Q5?

This offers no chance at all. Nor would 29. NxNP?, Q—N2!; 30. N—R6ch, K—R1; or 30. Q—K3, B—N3; Black winning a piece either way. Best was to dispense with heroics and play 29. Q—K1!, when 29. ..., P—N3?; would be feeble because of 30. RxB!, PxR; 31. NxQBP; once again giving White splendid play for the exchange. Much better is 29. ..., B—N3; 30. R—K5, and now perhaps 30. ..., Q—R4; 31. K—R1, R—B3; 32. B—N1, R—R3; when a plausible continuation could be 33. P—R4, PxP e.p.; 34. B—B3, NxB; 35. RxN, P—R7; 36. B—B2, BxN!; 37. R(3)xB, R(3)—Q3; and wins (38. N—Q3, B—Q4ch; or 38. R—Q3, RxR; 39. PxR, B—Q8).

29. ...,   B x B
30. N(3) x B

30. QxN, B—N3; 31. RxB! would cost less material, but White prefers to give up a whole piece for the sake of rather an amusing idea. Anyway, by this time he was so short on the clock that a sober assessment of chances was no longer possible.

30. ...,   N—N6
31. Q—K3   P x N
32. R x B   N x R
33. Q—N6

Intending to answer 33. ..., R—R1; with 34. B—B5, recovering the exchange and, though a piece down, retaining certain playing chances because of the weakness of all black pawns. However, Black can do better:

33. ...,   N—B5!
34. Q x R   N—B3

Catching the white Queen. Here White was so short of time that he failed to resign, but the rest is of no interest and given merely for the sake of the record: 35. QxRch, QxQ; 36. B—Q4, N—K5; 37. R—Q1, Q—Q3; 38. R—Q3, P—N3; 39. N—R2, P—R4; 40. N—N4, P—R5; 41. K—B1, PxP; 42. PxP, Q—R3; 43. K—N1, Q—R6; 44. B—B2, N(B)—Q7. Here White exceeded the time limit in lieu of resigning.

Game No. 28.

Whether or not to barter the substance of a clear positional advantage for the shadow of a sacrificial attack is not, perhaps, a matter of mastership or non-mastership, but rather of temperament. No doubt many masters have done the same and come to grief in the process, just as White does in the following game from a match between teams of Hesse and Westphalia at Rüsselsheim 1960. Chess is not governed by objective factors alone, and on the whole it is far more difficult to conduct the defence than the attack in a violent attacking position. Here, however, it is the defender who has everything under control and the attacker who falters. Perhaps a non-master should be a tiny bit less ambitious when facing the defence of a master.

Black: Dr. W. Lange.
Caro-Kann Defence.

1. P—K4	P—QB3
2. P—Q4	P—Q4
3. P—K5	B—B4
4. N—K2	P—K3
5. N—N3	B—N3
6. P—KR4	P—KR3
7. P—R5	B—R2
8. P—QB3	P—QB4
9. B—Q3	B x B
10. Q x B	N—QB3

The mixture as before — and Black follows Dreyer (game No. 4) in missing the accurate sequence starting with 10. ..., Q—N3. However, White is satisfied to lead back to the Pachman game instead of the sharper 11. B—K3.

11. O—O	P x P?

This, however, is no longer an inaccuracy but a serious positional error. The white QN — somewhat difficult to develop in this variation — now gets to his best square, QB3, and the white QP can be protected by the natural B—K3 instead of the clumsy R—Q1.

12. P x P	Q—N3
13. B—K3!	R—B1
14. N—B3	KN—K2

At this early stage Black has a lost position. The often-times Hesse champion, Walter Jäger, who did not play in the match, had picked this game for a demonstration to the large crowd of onlookers and, without waiting for my move, had suggested the methodical 15. N—R4!, followed by N—QB5 and P—KB4—B5 (naturally I was out of earshot). I fully appreciated the strength of this line but unfortunately also spotted a most interesting sacrificial attack which I could not resist.

15. N—N5!?	N—N5
16. Q—K2	N(2)—B3
17. P—R3	N—B7
18. QR—B1	N x B
19. P x N	P—R3
20. Q—KB2!	

The idea. At the cost of a piece White destroys the black centre and drives the King out into the open. The plan is no doubt correct — but proves too difficult for me to follow up correctly!

20. ...,	Q x N

There is nothing better. The KBP cannot be protected, and if he takes with the RP, he cannot protect the QP on move 22.

21. Q x P ch	K—Q1
22. Q x KP	K—B2
23. P—R4!	

This and the following move force Black to surrender the guard of the squares QN2 and QB3 when the attack should be decisive. The alternative for Black would be to give up the QP when the white centre pawns would become very dangerous and the N gains entry on K4.

23. ...,	Q—R4
24. P—K4	R—Q1
25. R—B7 ch	K—N3

The consequence of the moves P—R4 and P—K4: the black King cannot get back "home", for if 25. ..., K—N1?; 26. RxN!, PxR; 27. QxBP, and mate in a couple of moves.

26. P x P?

The decisive mistake. On the correct 26. N—B5! White feared the reply 26. ..., B—N5; 27. N—K3, B—Q7; failing to foresee the resource 28. RxNch!, PxR; 29. N—B4ch!, PxN; 30. Q—K7, R—Q2!; 31. QxR, QxRP;

66

32. Q—R7ch, K—R4!; and now 33. R—B3!, when it is doubtful whether Black can save himself. Other possibilities are simpler to deal with: 26. ..., B—N5; 27. N—K3, KR—K1; 28. NxPch, RxN; 29. RxPch, KxR; 30. QxNch, K—R2; 31. PxR, with four pawns for the piece and a powerful attack; or if 28. ..., QxN; 29. QxQ, RxQ; 30. PxR, NxQP; 31. R—QB4!, B—B4; 32. P—QN4!, N—K7 dis ch; 33. K—R2, B—Q5; 34. P—K6, B—B3; 35. K—R3! with the threat of R(4)—B7. Finally, if 26. ..., PxP; 27. N—K3, RxP; 28. Q—B8!

After the text the important square Q5 is laid bare too early.

26. ...,	**Q x QP**
27. P—R5 ch	**Q x P!**

Not 27. ..., KxP; 28. RxQNP! (threatening mate by R—R1ch, etc.), QxPch; 29. K—R2, Q—R5ch; 30. Q—R3!, and after the exchange of Queens the mating threat costs the N.

28. N—B5	**Q—Q4!**

Back to the pivot square!

29. Q—N6	**B—N5**
30. N—K3	

White is already satisfied with a draw: 30. ..., QxQP?; 31. RxPch!, KxR; 32. QxNch, and perpetual check. But Black has better.

30. ...,	**Q—N4!**
31. N—B5	**KR—B1!**
32. P—K6	**Q—Q4**

Again!

33. R x R

If immediately 33. P—K7, BxP!; 34. NxB, QxR; 35. RxNch!, K—R2!; 36. RxPch, PxR; 37. N—B6ch, K—R1; and wins. Or 33. RxNch, PxR; 34. P—K7, BxP; 35. NxB, QxPch; 36. K—R1, Q—R5ch; and wins. The game is lost.

33. ...,	**R x R**
34. P—K7	**B x P**
35. N x B	**Q x P ch**

White resigns, since Q—R5ch regains the piece.

It is disappointing to lose such a game, but this should not blind the reader to the fact that, from Black's point of view, he fully deserved to win as a reward for his impeccable defence in difficult circumstances. Not only does chess admit of two points of view — without two points of view there would be no chess.

Game. No. 29.

Combinations in defence are easily missed, both by the attacker and by the defender. Players short of master strength are too much inclined to equate defence with passivity, as I know only too well from sad experience. But sometimes one finds a way of not turning the other cheek . . . such as I found in the following game from the semi-finals of the German team championships 1960.

Black: H. de Carbonnel.
Sicilian Defence.

1. P—K4	P—QB4
2. N—QB3	N—QB3
3. P—B4	P—KN3
4. N—B3	B—N2
5. B—N5	P—Q3
6. P—Q3	

More consistent would be the immediate 6. BxN, to try and bring about the Wyvill Formation (see game

No. 5) if Black should ever advance the QP. White wants to give up the B for the QN anyway, since in his planned build-up this would be the "bad" Bishop.

6. ...,	B—Q2
7. B x N	B x B
8. O—O	N—R3

More pointed than the usual 8. ..., N—B3. Black intends to hit at the white centre at once .

9. Q—K1	Q—Q2
10. Q—R4	P—B4
11. B—Q2	O—O—O
12. N—Q5	QR—K1
13. B—B3	B x B
14. N x B	

The pride of the black game has met with an inglorious end, but even so White has no advantage. Black's remaining B will be strong and, based on its attacking potential, Black immediately opens files on the K-side, offering a pawn in the process. White accepts, confident that he can weather the storm.

14. ... ,	N—N5
15. KR—K1	P—KR3
16. R—K2	P—KN4?!
17. BP x P	RP x P
18. Q x P	QR—N1
19. Q—Q2!	

If 19. QxBP, QxQ; 20. PxQ, BxN; 21. PxB, NxP dis ch; 22. K—B2, R—R6; 23. R—K3, R(6)—N6!; with advantage. Against the text Black has prepared a seemingly decisive combination, but there is a snag!

| 19. ... , | P x P |

If 19. ... , P—K4; 20. P—KR3, Q—R2; 21. R—KB1, with the threat of 22. N—KN5, when RxBP and also, on occasion, PxN is in the offing.

20. N x P	N x P?
21. N x N	Q—R6
22. Q—B4	P—K4

If now 23. NxPch, K—N1 (simplest) and White can no longer guard both KN2 and KR2. But there is a simple "out".

See diagram opposite.

23. Q—B8 ch!

Black cannot even decline the "sacrifice", otherwise all his centre pawns fall and White still protects both KN2 and KR2 (playing his Q to K5). This is the work of the N on K4. If, on the other hand, Black had removed the N first, he would have created the defence, Q—B5ch.

Position after Black's 22nd move.

23. ... ,	R x Q
24. P x Q	K—B2
25. R—KB1	R x R ch
26. N x R	R x P
27. R—R2!	R x R
28. N x R	P—N3
29. K—B2	

With the exchange of both Rooks White has brought about a clearly won ending, but the process is not quite simple and rather interesting. White must first stabilize the position in the centre, then render the B immobile, and finally use his K to force the black Q-side pawns to advance, after which they will be captured.

| 20. ... , | P—B5 |

Trying to exchange as many pawns as possible, but White retains ample material for winning purposes.

30. N—B6	P x P
31. P x P	P—Q4
32. K—K3	K—Q3
33. P—Q4	P x P
34. K x P	K—B2
35. N—B3	B—N4

Naturally the QP cannot be held anyway and Black tries to have tempo moves with his B at his disposal.

36. N x P ch	K—N2
37. N—K5	B—B8
38. N—K3	B—R6
39. N(5)—N4	

Stalemating the Bishop. Now for the third part of the programme. Black, in his desire to keep the white K out of his vitals, will have to enter squares that enable the white N's to take up even more advantageous positions without allowing any freedom to the Bishop.

39.	...,	K—B3
40.	K—B4	P—R3
41.	K—N4?	

Pointless!

41.	...,	K—N2
42.	K—B4	K—B3
43.	K—Q4!	K—Q3
44.	N—B5 ch!	

If now 44. ..., K—K3; still 45. N(4)—K3, for the elimination of all pieces leaves an easily won pawn ending.

44.	...,	K—B3

45.	N(4)—K3	K—B2
46.	K—Q5	K—Q2
47.	N—Q4	K—B2
48.	N—K6 ch	K—N1

Another step forward, for 48. ..., K—Q2; 49. N—N5, would cost the Bishop.

49.	K—Q6	K—N2
50.	N—B8	P—N4

At last. Now it is all over.

51.	N—Q7	P—N5
52.	N—B4	B—B4
53.	N—R5 ch	K—B1
54.	N—N6 ch	K—N1
55.	N—Q5	K—R2
56.	K—B5	Resigns.

Game No. 30.

This game, played in the international tournament at Torremolinos 1961, is easily the worst in this collection. I have included it not only because my opponent is a very big fish, and not only because the sudden turn of events has its amusing side, but rather because of a blend of these two factors — to show how easy it is even for a grandmaster to go completely astray in a won position — not by a blunder or an oversight (which can happen to anybody) but in a sustained sequence of inferior moves. The game proves that as long as there are tactical chances on the board (as long, in other words, as the win cannot be guaranteed by sheer technique), one must not resign a battle against anybody.

White: M. Najdorf.
Dutch Defence.

1.	P—Q4	P—K3
2.	P—QB4	P—KB4
3.	P—KN3	N—KB3
4.	B—N2	B—K2

Once White has committed himself to an early P—QB4, there is no reason why Black should not adopt the sharper lines starting with B—N5ch.

5.	N—KB3	O—O
6.	O—O	P—Q3
7.	N—B3	Q—K1
8.	P—N3	QN—Q2?

A shockingly bad move with which Black aims at too much too early in the game. He does indeed advance his KP before White is ready to do likewise, but in a position in which

he is forced to recapture with the N instead of the P. Thus White will have a strong square at Q5 (a subsequent P—QB3 leaving the QP weak) and can also, on occasion, threaten the fatal break-through with P—QB5. White's build-up (aiming at B—QR3) is best countered with P—QR4, N—QR3 and N—QN5.

9.	B—QR3	P—K4
10.	N—QN5	B—Q1
11.	P x P	N x P
12.	P—K3	K—R1
13.	N x N!	

After the black K's move the white KB could not return to Q5 with check after the capture of the QNP. Black therefore threatened to develop his Q-side with B—Q2, because he would later be able to capture twice on QN4. By capturing immediately and then making a move which (a) contains a potential attack on Black's KBP and (b) prepares B—QN2, hitting the black Queen, White prevents this possibility and thus decisively impedes Black's development.

13. ...,	Q x N
14. Q—B2!	P—QR3
15. N—B3	Q—K1?

Having messed up his tempi, Black should now strive to develop his Q-side whatever the cost in time. Thus the modest 15. ..., QR—N1; would be far more purposeful than the text.

16. QR—Q1	Q—R4
17. N—K2	N—N5
18. P—R3	N—K4
19. N—B4	Q—R3

Black has been playing with the same two pieces all the time and is now hopelessly behind in development.

20. P—B5

Here the inevitable break comes and one should think the game is over.

| 20. ..., | N—B2 |
| 21. P x P | P x P |

Black has no choice. If 21. ..., NxP?; 22. N—Q5, P—B3; 23. BxN, QxB; 24. N—N6.

| 22. P—R4 | P—KN4! |

Objectively this move hardly deserves the exclamation mark — but then I wonder whether any move would in this melancholy position. But psychologically it presents a challenge. Black exposes his own King for the chance of also exposing that of his opponent — and, with the game hopelessly lost in the centre and on the Q-side, this is indeed the only chance he has.

As a result of Black's defiance, White wants to win quickly, and discards one positional winning line after the other for the sake of a knock-out blow. When the blow finally comes, it finds White at the receiving end.

| 23. P x P | B x P |
| 24. B—Q5 | |

Masking one of Black's weaknesses, the QP, and thus not unwelcome to Black.

| 24. ..., | N—K4 |
| 25. K—N2 | |

"Masking," so to speak, another of Black's weaknesses: for he can wish for nothing better than to have the white K exposed on a white square, so as to develop his QB with strong threats.

| 25. ..., | B—Q2!? |

Offering not only the NP but also the QR in case of 26. BxNP, QR—B1!; 27. BxR, RxB; 28. Q—N2, B—B3ch; when all black pieces would co-operate against the white K. On the strength of variations like these one can sense that the game enters a new phase: Black, though still lost, is coming back into the game.

| 26. R—KR1 | QR—B1!? |

All in the same style. White can now obtain a clearly won ending by 27. QxR! (but not 27. RxQ, RxQ; 28. RxQP, B—K2!; 29. RxB, BxB; with the threat of 30. ..., N—N5), and whether Black captures on B1 or R8, his QP falls without compensation. But White wants to win a piece — by pinning the black N, getting his own N away with tempo and then playing P—B4. What is more, he is perfectly right!

| 27. Q—N2 | Q—B3 |
| 28. N—R5! | |

The same story. White saw 28. BxQP, QxB; 29. QxNch!, QxQ; 30. N—N6ch, and 31. NxQ, but discarded it as giving too little, in view of his tremendous advantage.

28. ...,	Q—N3
29. P—B4!	B—KB3
30. N x B	R x N
31. B x QP?	

And now, when all is set, he finds a fly in the ointment: 31. PxN, P—B5!;

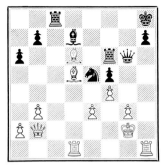

with the "unanswerable" double threat of 32. ..., QxPch; and 32. ..., R—B7ch. That at least was Black's intention and White's fear, but as the Munich player, E. Schiml, has pointed out, the threat was sheer bluff, for White would win at once with 32. RxPch! and now 32. ..., KxR; 33. R—R1ch, K—N2; 34. PxRch, etc., or 32. ..., QxR; 33. R—KR1, with heavy gain of material.

31. ...,   R x B
32. P x N?

This is really incomprehensible — alive to the danger of the move, P—B5, when it was imaginary, he now ignores it when it is real. White probably only saw the trap, 32. ..., RxB?; 33. P—K6ch, Q—N2; 34. QxQch, KxQ; 35. PxB, R—B7ch; 36. K—B3, and the QP costs the Rook, otherwise he could still have settled for a won ending with 32. QxNch, Q—B3; 33. BxP, R—B7ch; 34. K—B3, QxQ; 35. PxQ, RxR; 36. RxR, B—N4; 37. R—

Q8ch, etc.

32. ...,   Q—N2!

The pin has changed hands.

33. B x P   P—B5!

Leaving both Rooks *en prise*, but White's position is so strong that even this spectacular move is not yet sufficient to win the game.

34. P x P?

Only this loses. Threatened with 34. ..., QxPch; followed by the deadly check on QN4, White had to open square R1 for his K, and the sacrifice which in the variation on move 31 would have secured the win would now still obtain the draw: 34. RxPch!, KxR; 35. Q—N1ch! (but not immediately 35. RxR?, QxPch; 36. K—R1, Q—R6ch; 37. K—N1, R—N1ch; 38. B—N2, P—B6; 39. Q—B2ch, B—B4!; 40. Q—B7ch, K—R1; and wins), K—R1; 36. RxR, QxPch; 37. K—R1, Q—R6ch; 38. K—N1, and if now 38. ..., R—N1ch; 39. R—N6! Or 35. ..., R—N3; 36. BxR, BxB; 37. PxP.

34. ...,   B—R6 ch!

"Crafty, but elegant." (*Neue Zürcher Zeitung.*)

35. K—R2   R—R3
36. B x R   B—B8 dis ch
37. K—N1   Q x P ch
38. K x B   Q—B6 ch

Resigns — mate in three is unavoidable. Poor Don Miguel! "What a patzer I am!" was his disgusted comment.

Game No. 31.

Few games please both winner and loser. Here, played at the international tournament at Nathanya (Israel) 1961, is one that did. "You played a wonderfully imaginative defence," said Czerniak after the game, "and if I had not seen your game against Najdorf, I might have fallen for it".

White: M. Czerniak.
French Defence.

1. P—K4	P—K3
2. P—Q3	P—Q4
3. N—Q2	P x P?

This simplification in the centre comes much too early. It is the right policy if White should commit himself to either an early P—KB4 or the fianchetto of the KB — Black then aims at an open game with an early P—K4 and B—QB4. But at the present stage Black must adopt a more flexible policy and retain the option of a King's Indian set-up with colours reversed.

4. P x P	N—QB3
5. KN—B3	B—B4
6. P—B3	N—B3
7. B—K2	P—K4

Now this system is ineffective. With his pawns on K4 and QB3 White controls all important central squares; he will soon combine an attack against the KP with threats along the open Q-file.

8. O—O	O—O
9. Q—B2	P—QR3?

So as to retain the B on the QR2—KB7 diagonal where, however, it serves little purpose. Throughout the opening Black seems to think of the lines where White has played an early P—KB4.

10. N—B4	Q—K1

A choice of evils. If 10. ..., Q—K2; 11. P—QN4, B—R2; 12. B—N5, and Black cannot play P—QN4, because after 13. N—K3, BxN; 14. BxB, White controls the important square QB5. Meanwhile 13. P—QR4—QN5 is threatened.

11. P—QN4!	B—R2
12. P—QR4	B—N5!

Black, whose play has been very hazy up to this point, begins to sit up and take notice — better late than never. Faced, after White's P—QN5, with the double threat to his KP and his KR (by B—R3) he evolves a long combinational defence, branching out into a number of interesting variations, which only just fails.

13. P—N5	B x N
14. B x B	

The first point emerges after 14. PxB (so as to keep the N on B4 guarded against the threat that develops in the text). In this case Black is prepared to give up the exchange, for after 14. ..., N—Q1!; 15. B—R3, N—R4; 16. BxR, KxB; 17. N—K3, N—B5; 18. N—Q5, N(1)—K3; he has full value for the small material deficit.

14. ...,   **P x P**

Without this exchange White, it is true, would not have his brilliant 16th move available, but then he would not need it; after 14. ..., Q—K3; 15. B—K2!, N—Q1 (or K2 or N1); 16. B—R3, Black has no compensation for the pair of Bishops and other positional trumps. That the open R-file, which is part of Black's defensive combination, also benefits the opponent, is no more than poetic justice.

15. P x P   **Q—K3!**

16. R—R4!

The winning move, played after very long thought. If the tempting 16. PxN?, QxN; 17. PxP, BxPch; 18. QxB, RxR; 19. Q—N2, there would follow 19. ..., Q—B4ch; 20. K—R1, Q—R2! And if White interposes 16. B—R3, QxN; 17. BxR, N—Q5!; 18. Q—Q1, NxBch; 19. QxN, KxB; and though, after e.g. 20. P—N6, PxP; 21. R—R3, the black B will fall, Black will have at least two pawns for the exchange.

16. ...,	N—K2
17. Q—R2	N—B1
18. B—K3	P—QN3

Now Black is at the receiving end of the same tie-up as he enjoyed administering in the Euwe game (No.

72

15). But here he has at least some hope of getting his pieces out and without White's incisive conduct of the attack such hope might well have come to be realized.

19. Q—K2!

Unpinning his N and keeping the KN glued to his square because of the threat B—N4.

19. ...,	P—B3
20. R—N1	R—N1
21. P—N4!	

Masterly play — while Black is still busy disentangling his Q-side, his centre is assaulted from the other wing. The next five or six moves are a heroic fight to prevent B—N4 and the subsequent fall of the KP.

21. ...,	N—Q2
22. P—N5	P x P

The only reasonable try; if 22. ..., N—B4; the QNP runs amuck: 23. BxN, PxB; 24. R—R6!, Q—K1!; 25. P—N6, Q—Q1; 26. P—N7, QxPch; 27. K—R1, Q—K2; 28. N—R5 and wins.

23. R x P	Q—QB3
24. R(4)—N4	N—Q3

25. R—Q5!

Black has achieved the near-impossible, even to the extent of exchanging the powerful white N, but it is still not enough. In doing so, he had to allow the white R access to the 5th rank and the KP is as endangered as ever.

25. ...,	N x N
26. R x N(B4)	Q—N2
27. B—N4	

At last. Now Black, short of time and still intent on saving his KP, overlooks a final subtlety and allows a quickly decisive sacrificial attack. But with the fall of the KP the game was always lost.

27. ...,	P—B4(?)
28. Q—Q1!	

Enforcing BxBP.

28. ...,	N—B4
29. B x P	Q—R3
30. B x P ch!	K x B
31. Q—R5 ch	K—N1
32. P—N6	R—B5
33. Q—R7 ch	Resigns

— mate in a few moves is forced.

Game No. 32.

When Durao and I met at Habana 1966, we established a record: we became the first two players in the world to have met in tournament games in four Continents. Here is the Asiatic contribution to the total (Nathanya 1961).

White: J. Durao.
French Defence.

1. P—K4	P—K3
2. P—Q4	P—Q4
3. N—QB3	N—KB3
4. B—N5	B—K2
5. P—K5	KN—Q2
6. B x B	Q x B
7. P—B4	O—O
8. N—B3	P—QB4
9. B—Q3	P x P?!

Twice previously I had tried to get into this line. Gligoric at Torremolinos had avoided it by playing the theoretical 9. PxP, while the East German master, Liebert, in a friendly match between *Königsspringer* Frankfurt and *Chemie* Halle, had now tacked off with 10. N—QN5.

10. B x P ch?!	K x B
11. N—N5 ch	Q x N!

Forced, but, I believe, good.

12. P x Q	P x N
13. O—O	

See diagram on next page.

Nothing is known about this line. Keres mentions it in his book on the French, recommending 13. Q—Q3ch,

73

K—N1; 14. QxBP, but gives no material. Recent treatises (e.g. Schwarz's) quote the present game. All it proves, however, is that Durao's idea of carrying the attack with pieces only is inadequate and that White must throw his K-side pawns into the fray and therefore, presumably, refrain from O—O.

13. ...,	N x P
14. Q—R5 ch	K—N1
15. R—B4	N—N3
16. R—B3	P—K4!
17. P x P	

White must at last do something about this pawn, which Black had deliberately left all this time to be taken so as not to aid White in gaining open files for his Rooks. If he now plays 17. R(1)—KB1 (threatening 18. QxN, as well as 18. P—KN4), there would follow 17. ..., N—B5; 18. RxN, PxR; 19. RxP, PxP; 20. R—R4, P—N8(Q)ch; 21. K—B2, QxPch; 22. K—N3, Q—B6ch; 23. K—B2, Q—B4ch; and the mating threat is relieved by force, for if 24. K—B1, Q—B5ch!; if 24. K—N3, Q—K6ch; and if 24. K—B3, B—N5ch!

What then is White to do? If he captures with the R, simple development puts an end to the attack, the R missing from the natural KB-file. If he allows the P to live by P—QN3, it will later become a nuisance, though this might have been the least evil. In the game he captures with the

pawn, giving the black Rooks a wonderful file to work along.

17. ...,	N—B3
18. QR—KB1	B—K3!

Not only meeting the immediate threat of 19. QxN!, PxQ; 20. RxRch, K—R2; 21. R—K8! and wins, but also preparing for a cast-iron defensive set-up which leaves both his Rooks disengaged and ready to frolic on the QB-file.

19. P—N4!

At last White gets the time for this thematic move, but it comes too late. White hopes for 19. ..., N—B5?; 20. RxN, PxR; 21. R—B3!, KR—B1; 22. R—R3, K—B1; 23. Q—R8ch, K—K2; 24. QxP, with plenty of play.

19. ...,	QN—K2!
20. R—R3	KR—B1

Reaching the desired formation, in which the N on K2 defends his colleague after the black King has been forced onto the KB-file, and also stands ready to interpose on N1 against a Q sacrifice on R8.

21. Q—R7 ch	K—B1
22. R(3)—B3	R—B5
23. P—KR3	QR—B1

Since on, e.g. 24. R—B6?, Black can simply capture and continue the journey of his K, this is really the end of the attack, which now passes to Black. But the technical part still has interesting points.

24. R—K3	R x P
25. R x R	R x R
26. P—KR4	

A last fling to make the K-side pawns tell and a clever trap at the same time.

26. ..., R—N6 ch!

Killing it at once. If 26. ..., BxP; 27. P—R5, R—R6? (27. ..., R—N6 ch; is still alright); 28. PxN!, RxQ; 29. RxPch, and White wins! After the text the white K cannot go to B2 (27. K—B2, RxP; 28. P—R5, R—R5; 29. PxN, NxP!), so has to allow the R to

74

enter the R-file with the gain of a tempo.

27.	K—R2	R x P
28.	P—R5	R—R5 ch
29.	K—N1	N—B5
30.	P—R6	P x P
31.	Q—R8 ch!	

If first 31. PxP, N(2)—N3; 32. Q—N7ch, K—K2; the pawn cannot be held anyway and White does not even get the chance of "cleaning up" the Q-side.

31.	...,	N—N1
32.	Q x KP?	

But here 32. PxP, RxP; 33. QxP, is a little more accurate, since the N could then not be held on KB5 at Black's leisure. In the text Black has all the time in the world to weave an untearable mating net, based on the strength of this N.

32.	...,	P x P
33.	Q—N8 ch	K—N2
34.	Q x NP	N—B3
35.	Q x RP	P—Q5!

The threat N—K7ch protects the pawn and the white squares are cleared for the B to enter the game. After White's next move Black no longer allows a delay in the execution by a possible exchange sacrifice and goes straight for mate.

36.	P—R4	N—R6 ch
37.	K—R2	N—Q4
38.	P—R5	N—K6
39.	R—B3	N—B5 dis ch
40.	K—N1	R—N5 ch
41.	K—R2	

Or 41. K—B2, R—N7ch; 42. K—K1, R—K7 mate. If 41. K—R1, N—K7; threatening both B—Q4 and R—R5 mate.

41.	...,	R—N7 ch
42.	K—R1	R—Q7
43.	Q—K7	

and resigned simultaneously, realising that 43. ..., R—Q8ch; 44. K—R2, N—N5ch; 45. K—N3, R—N8 is mate. If instead 43. RxN(3), PxR; 44. QxP, B—Q4ch; 45. K—N1, R—N7ch; 46. K—B1, B—B5ch; 47. K—K1, R—K7ch finishes.

After this game one of the spectators came up to tell me that he had enjoyed this game more than any of those played at the great Zurich International tournament 1959, which he had watched from beginning to end. Matters of taste are unarguable — anyway, it is a pleasant feeling to have given so much satisfaction to somebody.

Game No. 33.

Consistency is not always a virtue in chess. Where your plan is faulty, sticking to it will certainly lose you the game, whereas swapping horses in midstream MIGHT save something from the wreck. It seems strange to find so many strong players adopt the opposite view, as e.g. my opponent in the following game from the international tournament at Imperia 1961.

Black: A. Magrin.
Sicilian Defence.

1.	P—K4	P—QB4
2.	P—QB3	P—Q4

The "classical" reply to the Alapin move, which I have always liked to play against. White has fewer problems than in the line beginning with 2. ..., N—KB3.

3.	P x P	Q x P

4.	P—Q4	N—KB3
5.	N—B3	N—B3
6.	B—K3	

In this line White is well advised to try for a simplification in the centre by forcing Black to BPxP, and thus to gain square QB3 for the N. What happens when Black tries to avoid PxP, was shown in a game Heidenfeld-Philpott, London league 1953, in which

Black had played 5. ..., B—N5; 6. B—K2, P—K3; 7. P—KR3, B—R4; 8. O—O, N—B3; 9. B—K3, and now 9. ..., R—Q1? There followed 10. PxP, BxP; 11. QxQ, RxQ; 12. P—B4!, BxN; 13. PxR, BxKB; 14. PxN, BxR; 15. PxP, K—Q2; 16. BxB, B—R3; 17. BxP, and White won the ending.

6. ...,	P x P
7. P x P	P—K3
8. N—B3	B—N5

The play against the QN is faulty and ultimately leads to Black's downfall.

9. B—Q3	Q—QR4
10. Q—B2	N—Q4

All with the same — unattainable — object.

11. B—Q2	B—Q2
12. O—O	R—QB1
13. P—QR3	

So far Black has been able to develop "normally" and, as it seemed, purposefully. Now this pleasant state of affairs comes to an end.

13. ...,	B x N?

After this move the white game plays itself. The white centre is strengthened, the black N on Q4 becomes subject to attack, and the black squares in Black's camp are fatally weakened. Much better was the retreat 13. ..., B—K2. Black probably saw the reply, 14. B—K4!, forcing yet another re-developing move, 14. ..., N—B3; and on 15. P—Q5(?), a third one, 15. ..., N—Q1. But after that, suddenly White does not seem to get any further, for the combination 16. P—Q6, BxP; 17. Q—Q3 (so as to threaten a discovered attack on the black Queen, while her white colleague gets out of the pin), can be answered with 17. ..., B—K2; 18. N—Q5, PxN!; 19. BxQ, PxB; 20. Q—K3, N—B3!; 21. B—N4, PxN!; 22. BxB, N—Q4!; and Black retains three minor pieces for the Queen.

After 13. ..., B—K2!; 14. B—K4, N—B3; the correct move is 15. N—Q5!, Q—Q1; 16. NxNch, BxN (not 16. ..., PxN; 17. B—B3, P—B4?; 18. BxP!, PxB; 19. P—Q5, with an overwhelming game); 17. Q—Q3, and White has a clear positional advantage, though the resultant position would still require a great deal of work. But Black cannot put up with the "humiliation" of getting nothing out of the demonstration against the Knight — hence the text move.

14. P x B	Q—B2
15. QR—N1	P—KR3
16. P—B4	N—B3

Black is still committed to this series of retreats — on top of all the drawbacks mentioned in the previous note. If now 16. ..., N—B5? (or 16. ..., N—N3; 17. Q—N3, N—Q1; 18. B—R5); 17. BxN, QxB; 18. RxP, NxP; 19. NxN, QxN; 20. R—Q1, B—B3; 21. RxBP!, and wins (21. ..., Q—N5; 22. P—B3).

17. Q—N2!

Threatening to rip open the centre by P—Q5.

17. ...,	N—Q1
18. P—Q5	P—QN4

A desperate expedient. 18. ..., O—O; would be refuted by 19. BxP, PxP; 20. B—N5!, PxP; 21. BxN, NPxB; 22. QxBP, PxB; 23. Q—N5ch, and 24. R—N4.

19. KR—B1	NP x P
20. B x BP	Q—Q3

21. N—K5

On the immediate 21. B—N4, Black could gain a move by 21. ..., Q—B5. Now there is no hope left, for if 21. ..., NxP; 22. NxB, KxN; 23. QxP.

21. ...,	P x P
22. B—N4	Q—N3
23. Q—K2	Q—K3

The alternatives are no better: (a) 23. ..., PxB; 24. NxB dis ch, Q—K3; 25. NxNch, PxN; 26. Q—R5. Or (b) 23. ..., N—K3; 24. NxB, KxN; 25. R—Q1! (simplest — if now 25. ..., K—B3; 26. B—K7). White merely has to guard against unwarranted brilliancy, such as 23. ..., N—K3; 24. B—N5?, RxRch; 25. RxR, QxB?; 26.

R—B8ch!, N—Q1; 27. N—B6 dis ch, and wins, for 25. ..., BxB!; would put a nasty end to the sweet dreams, for if then 26. R—B8ch, N—Q1; 27. N—B4 dis ch, N—K5!

24. B—N5   R x R ch

Or 24. ..., B—B3; 25. RxB, NxR; 26. R—QB1, respectively 24. ..., N—B3; 25. NxB, KxN; 26. RxN!, RxR (26. ..., QxQ; 27. R—Q6 dbl ch); 27. BxRch, and now if 27. ..., QxB; 28. Q—K7ch, K—B1; 29. B—Q2!, and if 27. ..., KxB; 28. Q—R6ch, etc.

25. R x R	B x B
26. Q x B ch	N—Q2
27. R—K1	P—R3
28. Q—R4	P—QR4
29. N x N	**Resigns.**

Game No. 34.

When you are faced with the prospect of a statically inferior game that is the time to throw whatever dynamic advantage you may have at the moment, into the scales. This is by no means "tactical" versus "positional" play, but tactical means to serve a positional end. A most exciting example, with the typical ebb and flow of such positions, occurred in my game against Wade at Enschede 1961.

White: R. G. Wade.
Slav Defence (in effect).

1. P—Q4	N—KB3
2. P—KN3	P—Q4
3. B—N2	P—KN3
4. N—KB3	B—N2
5. O—O	O—O
6. P—B4	P—B3
7. P x P	P x P

The game has become the Slav Exchange Variation with a double K-side fianchetto — a line of play frequently adopted in the Smyslov-Botvinnik match 1957.

8. N—B3	N—B3
9. N—K5	P—K3
10. B—B4	

Larsen (against Krogius, Le Havre 1966) preferred the immediate 10. NxN, PxN; 11. N—R4, when, after 11. ..., N—Q2; 12. B—B4, Black did not have the strong counter-play that

follows in the game. Perhaps 11. ..., N—Q2; should be replaced by 11. ..., Q—K2; keeping the option of employing the N on the K-side.

10. ...,	N—KR4!
11. N x N	P x N
12. B—K3	

Black has allowed the opponent to give him a backward P in an open file and unless he takes strong measures at once, White will now systematically exploit the QB-file and the strong square QB5. But the B is clumsily placed on K3 and a counter-attack against White's KB4 square suggests itself. It would be wrong to reason that the advance of the black KBP would weaken K3 and thus give added power to a white N on QB5 — the correct objective is to see that it does not get there!

| 12. ..., | P—KB4! |

13. Q—Q2	**R—N1**
14. N—R4	**Q—Q3**
15. QR—B1	

If now 15. ..., P—B5; 16. BxBP, NxB; 17. PxN, QxP; 18. QxQ, RxQ; 19. P—K3, and White gets very much the game he envisaged — this is how the position looks to White. But things are not quite what they seem. Nor could he interpolate 15. P—B4, because of 15. ..., Q—N5!

15. ...,	**P—B5!**
16. P x P?	

A curious double oversight. Neither White nor Black noticed in the heat of battle that Black could now get the advantage by 16. ..., B—KR3! The B had to capture first so as to reach the game continuation by force.

16. ...,	**N x P?**
17. B x N	**R x B!**

If now 18. P—K3, R—R5; 19. P—B4, P—N4!; when 20. Q—KB2?, would not do because of 20. ..., R—QN5; 21. N—B5, RxBP!; while even after 20. Q—K1, B—B3; White is in great difficulties. But he has prepared a little combination.

18. R x P!	**R x QP!**

So has Black! White had intended 18. ..., QxR; 19. QxR, R—N5; 20. R—B1!, Q—K1; 21. P—N3! Now Black cannot regain the pawn by 21. ..., BxP?; 22. P—K3, B—N7; 23. RxB!, or 22. ..., B—B6(B4); 23. Q—

QB7, winning a piece either way; nor by 21. ..., RxQP; 22. Q—QB7, B—R3; 23. P—K3, R—N5; 24. QxP.

19. R x Q

There is nothing better. 19. Q—B2, Q—Q1; gives White no advantage.

19. ...,	**R x Q**
20. R—Q8 ch	**K—B2**
21. R—B1	**R—N5!**

Not only saving the piece, but with a little nastiness in mind: if now 22. R—B7ch? (so as to force the black K to an unfavourable square), K—B3; 23. R(8)xB, there would follow 23. ..., R—B8ch; 24. B—B1, R—N5ch; 25. K—R1, RxB mate. A mate in which one Rook acts vertically and the other horizontally is somewhat unusual and may easily be overlooked — in fact, Wade afterwards claimed having been saved from it only by the timely arrival of his supper. It is obvious that we were too well looked after at Enschede!

22. N—B5	**B x P**
23. R—N1	**R—N1**
24. N—Q3	

Threatening to win a piece by 25. NxB. Suddenly the black pieces have got into a complete bind, which allows only one answer:

24. ...,	**K—K2**
25. R—N8	**K—B2!**
26. R—Q8	**K—K2**

and my offer of a draw was accepted. White has as little choice as Black, for if 27. R—R8, BxR; 28. RxR, R—B7; while the "win" of two pieces for a Rook by 27. RxQB, RxR; 28. RxB (28. NxR?, R—QN1), RxR; 29. NxR, would be suicidal.

A somewhat slight game (and a little devalued by the double oversight on move 16), but its merit is that the combinational sequence is the logical answer to Black's need of foiling the opponent's plans on the QB-file.

Game No. 35.

Played in the Frankfurt league matches of 1962, this game was a farewell performance for both players. It was my last appearance for *Königsspringer* prior to my return to Dublin, and my opponent's last game for *Schachfreunde* before returning to his native Austria, for which he had played, with considerable success, at the Munich Olympic team tournament 1936 and such strong international events as the Bad Gastein tournament 1948.

White: Dr. R. Palme.

Double Fianchetto.

1.	N—KB3	N—KB3
2.	P—QN3	P—KN3
3.	B—N2	B—N2
4.	P—N3	P—Q4
5.	P—B4	P—B3
6.	B—N2	O—O
7.	O—O	QN—Q2
8.	P—Q3	R—K1
9.	N—B3	P—K4
10.	P—K4	P—Q5

Against his opponent's slow and artificial build-up Black has made simple sensible moves with the result that often happens in a double fianchetto: one of White's Bishops is hemmed in by his own pawns, the other by the opponent's pawns. It is clear at this early stage that Black has nothing to worry about.

11.	N—K2	N—B1
12.	B—B1	N—R4
13.	N—R4	

So as to stop the advance of the KBP for the time being.

13.	...,	B—B3
14.	N—KB3	B—N2
15.	N—K1?	

White is certainly not so well placed that he should go out of his way to avoid a repetition of moves and might well have waited for Black to invent something more convincing than B—B3. After the text his pieces will barely have standing room.

15.	...,	P—KB4
16.	P—B3	Q—Q3
17.	P—QR4	P—QR4
18.	R—R2!	

An important defensive measure in many variations. With the whole of the bottom rank crammed full with idlers, this is the only way for the Rook to make itself useful.

18.	...,	P—B5
19.	P x P	P x P
20.	K—R1	P—KN4
21.	N—N1	

Six white pieces on the bottom rank, two on the second. No wonder Black threatens mate on the move with his next.

21.	...,	Q—R3
22.	B—KR3	N—N3

At first glance one thinks that 22. ..., BxB; 23. NxB, N—N6ch; 24. PxN, QxNch; would win at once. But after 25. K—N1, the position is far from clear, e.g. 25. ..., QxPch; 26. R—N2, Q—R6; 27. RxP, and the white pieces are freed for the defence. Or 25. ..., PxP; 26. BxP!, P—R3 (26. ..., R—K4; 27. P—B4, P—R3; 28. PxR, PxB; 29. Q—B3, is good for White); 27. B—B1!, R—K4; 28. Q—K2, R—R4; 29. Q—N2, Q—R5; 30. P—B4! However this may be, I could not see anything clear, and in that case it must be right on principle not to allow White to ease the congestion of his pieces.

23.	K—N2	N—K4
24.	B x B	KR x B!

This Rook has no function at the moment, whereas the other R guards the RP. Thus after 24. ..., QRxB; 25. B—Q2, R—R1; White might activate his Q-side by P—N4.

25.	R(1)—B2	N—B3
26.	K—B1	B—B1
27.	R—KN2	K—B2(?)

But this is automatic play. Black does not realise in time that after his opponent's *riposte* the KB-file will be just as important as the KN-file (square KB5!) and that his K would have been better placed on R1.

28. P—R4!?

An ingenious attempt to break Black's strangle-hold. All white pieces suddenly find squares. That it does not quite succeed is due to the fact that the position is too bad by this time.

28. ...,	P x P
29. N—R3	N—R4
30. R—N5	N—N6 ch
31. K—N1	N—N3
32. N—N2	B—Q3
33. R—N4	R—KN1
34. K—B2	QR—KB1!

A position that might have come from the hand of a puzzle composer, with the stipulation: can, or cannot, White take the BP, and if so, how? Clearly the R cannot take, White getting no compensation for the exchange, nor can the B, because after NxB the vital R on N4 would be attacked.

35. N(2) x BP?

The answer is that the P is taboo. As for capturing with this N and following up with the other N, see the game. If, however, 35. ..., BxN; 36. BxB, there could follow: 36. ..., NxB; 37. RxNch, K—K2; 38. RxR

(if 38. Q—Q2, Q—K3!; 39. RxR, QxN; with a mating threat on KB8, and if 38. Q—QB1, Q—N3; 39. RxR, NxPch!; 40. QPxN, Q—N7ch; 41. K—K1, Q—R8ch; 42. K—Q2, R—N7ch; followed by QxQ), Q—K6ch; 39. K—N2, RxR (stronger than 39. ..., KxR; 40. K—R2!); and the white position is hopeless.

But why not capture with the other N, seeing that 35. N(3)xP, NxN; 36. BxN, BxB; 37. RxBch, K—K2; 38. RxP, with the surviving N guarding both KR4 and K3, seems very dubious. The refutation is as surprising as it is logical — for what could be more surprising than a "slow" Q sacrifice and what more logical than the free RP's "lust to expand"? Thus: 35. N(3)xP, P—R6!!; 36. NxN, QxN!; 37. RxQ, RxR; 38. N—R4, P—R7; 39. NxR, P—R8(Q); 40. QxQ, NxQch; 41. K—N2, KxN; 42. P—B4! (42. KxN?, RxP; with the double threat of R—B8ch and RxP), BxP; 43. BxB, RxB; 44. KxN, R—B6; 45. R—Q2, K—N4; 46. K—N2, R—K6; and wins the R ending. And if, in this line, 37. N—B4, P—R7!; 38. NxQ, RxN; 39. RxN, BxRch; 40. K—K2 (if 40. K—N2, B—B5 dis ch, and Black remains a piece up), B—K8!; 41. QxB, R—N8 and wins.

I certainly did not see any of this during the game; nor can I believe that my opponent, in the throes of extreme time pressure, did. If I am wrong, this is one more example of not seeing the wood for the trees, for the denouement he chooses is the most immediately fatal one of all. More likely he did not want to free the RP as a matter of principle.

35. ...,	B x N
36. N x B?	N—K4!

That this N stays alive is immediately decisive.

| 37. R x R | K x R |

38. N—R3		38. . . . ,	Q x B!
Since 38. N—K2, is answered by		39. Q x Q	N x P ch
38. . . . , RxPch.		Resigns.	

Game No. 36.

Immortality is as difficult to attain at chess as in any other field. "Negative immortality" is somewhat easier, though even this is difficult enough — who loses games of the calibre Rotlevi did against Rubinstein, Napier did against Lasker, or Zubarev did against Capablanca? The following most amusing game, played at the I.B.M. tournament Amsterdam 1962, will probably rot in the archives because I happened to handle the intriguing complications correctly. If I had slipped on move 23, I might have joined the "negative immortals" — two successive Queen sacrifices IN DEFENCE are certainly sufficiently unusual to be remembered. Most unfair!

White: J. H. Donner.
Slav Defence.

1. P—Q4	P—Q4
2. P—QB4	P—QB3
3. N—KB3	N—B3
4. N—B3	P x P
5. P—QR4	P—K3

Soultanbeieff's idea: if now 6. P—K4, P—QB4; 7. P—Q5, NxKP?!; 8. NxN, PxP; 9. N—B3, B—K3; with double-edged play.

| 6. P—K3 | B—N5 |
| 7. B x P | Q—R4? |

Inaccurate — this move should be preceded by 7. . . . , QN—Q2; only after White threatens to advance P—K4 (by; say, Q—K2 or Q—B2), is the Q-move indicated. The difference will be shown in the next note.

| 8. B—Q2 | QN—Q2 |
| 9. P—K4(?) | |

Much better is first 9. O—O, and if then 9. . . . , O—O; 10. Q—N3, as Dr. Filip played against me at Enschede 1963. Then Black can no longer play 10. . . . , P—K4; because the black Q has to support the B; nor could Black have played the immediate 9. . . . , P—K4; 10. PxP, NxP; 11. NxN, QxN; 12. Q—N3, and wins a pawn. With the white K still in the centre, this play against Black's KBP allows dubious complications.

9. . . . ,	P—K4!
10. P x P	QN x P
11. N x N	Q x N
12. Q—N3	

And not 12. BxPch?, KxB; 13. Q—N3ch, N—Q4!; and Black keeps his piece no matter how White wriggles. Nor could White have played 10. Q—N3, at once, i.e. without the exchanges in the centre, for Black would cheerfully have given up the KBP by 10. . . . , PxP!; securing the square QB4 for his N.

| 12. . . . , | B x N |

After 12. . . . , NxP?; 13. BxPch, would be strong; if then 13. . . . , K—B1; 14. QxBch, N—Q3 dis ch; 15. B—K3, White has much the better development.

13. B x B!

Winning the exchange, at a price. The alternative, 13. BxPch, K—B1; 14. BxB, QxPch; 15. K—B1 (not 15. K—Q1?, B—N5ch; 16. P—B3, BxPch; 17. PxB, QxPch; 18. K—B2, Q—K5 ch! etc.), is best answered with 15. . . . , P—QN3!, allowing the defence P—QB4 on B—N4ch and giving the chance of B—R3ch in turn. 15. . . . , N—Q4!; 16. BxN, QxB (on 16. . . . , PxB; 17. R—Q1 is unpleasant); 17. QxQ, PxQ; on the other hand, would leave White with a clear advantage.

81

13. ...,	Q x P ch
14. K—B1	O—O
15. B—N4	

Stopping the threat of B—R6, which can now be answered with P—B3, and threatening the exchange. But Black is quite happy to oblige.

15. ...,	B—B4
16. P—B3	Q—B5
17. B x R	R x B
18. R—Q1!	

A very fine move, which not only threatens to win a pawn by 19. BxPch, but also prepares for the development of the KR — P—KN3 can now be played, since the K can enter KB2 without being checked on Q5.

18. ...,	N—N5!?

Here I considered 18. ..., P—KN3 (P—KN4 may be more forceful); but the weakness of KB3 is unpleasant, e.g. 19. Q—B3! (not yet threatening QxN, but getting ready for it), N—K5; 20. Q—B1!, or 19. ..., N—N5; 20. K—N1! I decided that this was too slow and offered my BP into the bargain.

19. B x P ch	K—R1
20. P—N3?	

In keeping with Donner's plan, but not the strongest. I was worried about 20. Q—R3!, when after 20. ..., Q—N1!; 21. PxN, BxP; 22. R—K1! (but not 22. R—Q2?, Q—B5ch; 23. K—N1, QxB; 24. P—R3, Q—B8ch; 25. K—R2, Q—B5ch), Q—B5ch; 23. K—N1, QxB; Black would have virtually no hope for a draw. Even worse would be the alternative, 20. ..., B—Q6ch?; 21. RxB!, QxB; 22. Q—N3!, e.g. 22. ..., Q—KB5; 23. P—N3, Q—K5?; 24. R—Q8! (24. ..., Q—N8ch; 25. K—N2, N—K6ch; 26. QxN, QxPch; 27. Q—Q2).

20. ...,	Q—B2!

Of course not 20. ..., NxPch?; 21. K—N2.

21. P x N

What else? If 21. K—N2, B—B7.

If 21. K—N1, RxB!; 22. QxR?, QxQ; 23. R—Q8ch, Q—N1; 24. RxQch, KxR; 25. PxN, B—K5; and Black wins the pawn ending.

21. ...,	B—K5!
22. R—KN1!	

Played with extraordinary sangfroid, which is quite typical of Donner. As shown above, 22. K—N1, left Black with all the chances, since White must not exchange Q and R.

22. ...,	R x B ch!

Not first 22. ..., B—Q4; because of 23. RxB — with the K still on B1 he can reach the haven of KR3 (and certainly not 22. ..., B—Q4; 23. RxB!, QxBch??; 24. R—B5, QxQ; 25. RxRch).

23. K—K1	B—Q4!

The best move in the game. Of course White threatened 24. QxR, but could that not have been parried with 23. ..., R—B6; 24. Q—K6, Q—R4 ch!; 25. R—Q2 (25. K—K2, Q—R3 ch; leads to mate), R—K6ch!; and Black wins the Q by a discovered check without allowing mate on the back rank? But, alas, White would have answered 23. ..., R—B6?; with 24. R—KB1!, Q—R4ch; 25. K—K2!, Q—R3ch; 26. Q—N5!, and wins.

24. Q—Q3!

Again very fine. If the "natural" 24. Q—QB3?, Q—K2ch; 25. K—Q2, Q—N4ch!; 26. K—B2, B—K5ch; and if now 27. K—N3, Black has the time to pick up the Q by 27. ..., R—B6;

82

without allowing mate. Nor is 24. RxB, feasible any longer because of 24. ..., PxR; 25. QxQP, Q—B8ch.

24. ...,   Q—K4 ch

Making an end of the excitement. After the game the quiet 24. ..., Q—R4ch; 25. Q—B3, QxP; collecting another Q-side pawn, was suggested, but after 26. R—N2!, White rallies his Rooks and would have the better chances.

25. Q—K2	Q x Q ch
26. K x Q	B—B6 ch
27. K—K3	B x R
28. R x B	R—K2 ch

29. K—B4

Hereabouts I offered a draw, but Donner decides to play about a little. The position is dead drawn — if in the final position of the actual game the white K runs to hide at KR4, Black merely plays the R back to the second rank. The remaining moves were: 29. ...., K—N1; 30. P—R4, K—B2; 31. R—Q8, P—B4; 32. R—QB8, P—QN3; 33. P—N5, K—K3; 34. P—KR5, R—Q2; 35. R—K8ch, K—B2; 36. R—QB8, K—K3; 37. P—KN4, P—N3; 38. P—R6, R—Q5ch; 39. K—B3, R—Q6ch; 40. K—B4, R—Q5ch — draw agreed.

Game No. 37.

Simplicity can be very deceptive at chess. In the following game, played on the occasion of a match between Oxford University and Dublin in 1964, the moves seem "to play themselves" and the whole business takes only 24 of them. Yet the planning of the game required a great deal of unconventional — in fact, anti-conventional — thought, and it is because of this feature that I have included this slight game in the collection.

Black: P. N. Lee.

French Defence, Alapin Gambit(?).

1. P—K4	P—K3
2. P—Q4	P—Q4
3. B—K3	P—KB4?!

A most unusual reply, doing away with any thought of gambitry, which is perfectly playable.

4. P x BP	P x P
5. N—KB3	N—KB3
6. B—Q3	B—Q3
7. N—K5	O—O
8. P—KB4	P—B4?

This somewhat premature attempt at breaking up the white centre by means of a temporary P sacrifice gives the game its face. Though having castled, Black is really the opening tempo behind in an essentially symmetrical position — little wonder the time for violence has not come.

9. P x P!

The way to refute Black's idea is to play along with it. White is ready to have all the centre pawns removed and give up his pair of Bishops into the bargain (though traditionally the Bishops should be most powerful on an open board). He will then emerge with a useful lead in development and have ready targets in Black's remaining centre pawns.

9. ...,	B x N
10. P x B	N—N5
11. Q—Q2	N—QB3
12. O—O!	N(3) x P

Attacking gestures like 12. ..., Q—R5; 13. P—KR3, N(3)xP?; 14. PxN, NxP; 15. B—B4, P—KN4; 16. P—KN3, are doomed to failure.

13. P—KR3!

Forcing the very simplification Black is playing for. 13. B—KB4, could be answered with 13. ..., Q—K2; when White must waste a precious developing tempo to defend the BP. And on

83

13. B—Q4?, Q—B2! threatens all of NxB, NxP, and N—QB3, while the reply 14. BxN loses a pawn after 14. ..., QxPch.

13. ...,	N x QB
14. Q x N	N x B
15. Q x N	

The position White had in mind. The white N will be easily developed while the black B will be very bad. If Black tries to make it good by 15. ..., P—Q5; this pawn falls at once after 16. R—B4, R—K1; 17. N—Q2. Or, again, 15. ..., P—B5; 16. N—B3, P—Q5; 17. Q—B4ch, K—R1; 18. QR—Q1.

15. ...,	P—QN3
16. N—B3	P—Q5

A choice of evils. The B cannot go to N2 because of the KBP, and 16. ..., B—K3; is not a move one would make with any relish.

17. QR—Q1	B—K3

Position after White's 20th move.

18. Q x QP	Q x Q
19. R x Q	P x P
20. R—Q6!	

See diagram opposite.

The outcome of the adventure started with 8. ..., P—B4. Black has weaknesses everywhere and the "long-striding" B has virtually no square, which comes out best after 20. ..., B—B5; 21. R—B4.

20. ...,	KR—K1

Or 20. ..., K—B2; 21. R—K1, KR—K1; 22. N—Q5, BxN (22. ..., QR—Q1?; 23. R(1)xB!); 23. RxR, RxR; 24. RxB, and wins one of the BP's.

21. N—Q5	QR—Q1?

This loses either a whole piece or two pawns. 21. ..., KR—Q1; would have kept the loss to one pawn after 22. N—K7ch, K—B2; 23. NxP, RxR! (but not 23. ..., BxP?; 24. R—QR6, B—Q4; 25. P—B4!, and there is no room for the B on the wide open board!); 24. NxRch, K—K2; 25. N—B5ch, but the ending offers little hope. Black must then either exchange the B just when it might at last be of some use, or, after 25. ..., K—Q2; let go of the NP, when all his pawns will be weak and isolated.

22. N—K7 ch!	K—B2
23. N x P	B x P
24. R—QR6	Resigns

for he cannot parry the double threat of RxB and N—Q6 dbl ch.

Game No. 38.

Almost every tournament player remembers events where everything seemed to go just right for him. For me, one of these pleasant occasions was the Leinster Championship 1965, an exceptionally strong event by Irish standards and one in which at least five of my eight games contained interesting points and were of publishable standard. The best of these was undoubtedly the following:

Black: E. A. Keogh.		
QP, Torre Opening.		
1. P—Q4	P—Q4	
2. N—KB3	N—KB3	
3. B—N5	P—K3
4. P—K3	P—B4
5. P—B3	N—B3
6. B—Q3	

This opening is often referred to as a Colle System with previously-developed QB. This is what it looks like, but the ideas behind either opening are quite different. With the QB locked in at home, White will always continue with P—K4 at an opportune moment; with the QB developed, he may do so, but actually has a wide choice, such as a later P—QB4 or even a Stonewall with N—K5 and P—KB4.

| 6. ..., | P x P? |

A very inferior exchange in this type of position. It is clear that the half-open K-file will be much better value for White than the half-open B-file for Black; a K-side attack will soon be in the offing, while the minority attack on the other wing is a remote possibility for Black.

| 7. KP x P | B—Q3? |

And this costs an additional tempo. Black will be unable to unscramble his pieces without killing the pin of his KN (see move 10) and should have played 7. ..., B—K2.

8. O—O	O—O
9. R—K1	P—KR3
10. B—R4	B—K2
11. QN—Q2	P—R3

A mere tempo count shows that White is two developing moves ahead, but this is not the whole extent of his advantage: Black's QB will be difficult to develop without getting into the way of other pieces, and White's half-open file is worth more than the one Black will — eventually — be able to occupy in return.

12. Q—K2	R—K1
13. N—K5	N x N
14. P x N	N—Q2
15. B x B	Q x B
16. N—B3	N—B4
17. N—Q4!	

The KB need not be preserved — at worst White will play an ending of N vs. bad B. If Black pushes the Q-

side pawns, as happens in the game, so as to give the B scope, a K-side attack will develop almost of its own accord. And if Black refuses to exchange White, after developing the QR, will play B—N1 and Q—QB2, creating further attacking chances.

17. ...,	N x B
18. Q x N	B—Q2
19. P—KB4	QR—B1
20. R—K3	P—QN4
21. QR—K1	Q—B4

With this move Black allows the coming attack, believing that he can always break it by a timely exchange of Queens (in the diagrammed position). The strategic alternative was 21. ..., P—B4; 22. PxP e.p., QxP; 23. P—B5, PxP (if 23. ..., P—K4; 24. N—B3, wins a pawn); 24. RxRch, RxR; 25. RxR, BxR; 26. QxP, when he has to submit to a long and most unpromising end-game requiring unceasing vigilance and probably lost even then.

| 22. P—QR3! | |

Not so much in order to stop P—N5 as to free the Queen for action without losing the QP.

22. ...,	Q—B5
23. Q—Q1!	P—QR4
24. Q—N4	K—R2

If 24. ..., K—R1; 25. R—N3, R—KN1; 26. Q—N5!, threatening Q—K7.

| 25. R—N3 | R—KN1 |
| 26. N—B3 | |

Now the threat of 27. N—N5ch, cannot be parried by 26. ..., B—K1; 27. N—N5ch?, K—R1!; because White would interpolate 27. Q—R3, threatening P—B5. Black cannot remove the nuisance by 27. ..., QxKBP?; 28. R—N4, Q—B4; 29. N—Q4, losing the Queen, so still has to submit to the weakening P—N3.

| 26. ..., | P—N3(?) |

But after this fatal weakening Black is demonstrably lost. He had to try 26. ..., Q—B4ch; 27. K—R1, Q—K2;

at this point.

27.	Q—R4	K—N2
28.	R—R3	P—R4
29.	Q—B6 ch	K—B1
30.	N—N5	Q—B4 ch
31.	R(1)—K3	Q—K2

Black no doubt thought that he was still in time to exchange Queens and break the white attack. He is right in the first surmise, but as to the second, his troubles are just beginning!

32. P—KN4! **R—B5**

Realising that passive defence is hopeless. If 32. ..., PxP; 33. R—R7, QxQ; 34. PxQ, B—K1; 35. RxKP!, R—B2 (otherwise 36. R—K7); 36. R—K5!, threatening not only N—K6 ch and RxQP, but above all 37. RxP ch!, with mate on R7 or K6 according to which piece Black captures with — a double setting of the finish of the well-known game Pfleger-Domnitz, Tel Aviv Olympiad 1964. Or 32. ..., QxQ; 33. N—R7ch! (33. PxQ, R—B5!; is not quite clear), K—K2; 34.

NxQ, R—N2; 35. PxP, PxP dis ch; 36. R(R3)—N3! (better than the other R, when Black gets counter chances with P—N5), RxRch; 37. PxR. Now the black KRP is doomed, for after 37. ..., R—KR1; the K himself walks down the KR-file; and if the desperate 37. ..., P—R5; 38. PxP, R—B5; 39. P—R5, RxKBP; 40. R—R3, and the white pawn marches through. Finally, 32. ..., K—K1; also costs the KRP.

33.	P x P	P x P
34.	R(K)—N3	K—K1
35.	N—K4!	R x R ch
36.	R x R	

Threatening the problem mate 36. ..., QxQ; 37. R—N8ch, K—K2; 38. PxQ mate.

36.	...,	K—Q1
37.	R—N8 ch	B—K1
38.	Q x Q ch!	

This is now more accurate than the immediate 38. N—Q6, QxQ; 39. PxQ, RxKBP; because the P is much easier to defend on K5 than on B6.

38.	...,	K x Q
39.	N—Q6	Resigns.

For if 39. ..., RxKBP (to give the exchange rather than the piece offers no hope at all); 40. RxBch, K—Q2; 41. R—KB8, R—N5ch; 42. K—B2, R—N4; 43. RxPch, K—B3; 44. R—B4! (the final pleasantry), RxP; 45. N—B7, and the black R has no square and must be exchanged.

Game No. 39.

On the whole, tactical alertness is even more imperative in defence than in attack — or, in other words, it is easier to conduct the attack in accordance with general principles than the defence. As a result, in a hard-fought drawn game the defender is usually pleased with the outcome, feeling that he has been playing his hardest; the attacker will usually have a vague feeling that, as a result of his initiative, he might have done better here or could have improved there. This applies even more when the defender only needs a draw, as in the following game from the final round of the same event as game No. 38, where a draw was sufficient for me to win the tournament.

White: M. F. Littleton.

French Defence.

1. P—K4	P—K3
2. P—Q3	P—Q4
3. N—Q2	N—KB3
4. KN—B3	P x P

The same inferior treatment as in game No. 31, even though delayed by one move. However, my opponent treats it less accurately than Czerniak.

5. P x P	B—B4
6. B—Q3	N—B3
7. O—O	P—K4
8. B—N5	

It is clear that the double movement of the B gives Black time for essential defensive measures.

8. ...,	B—KN5
9. P—KR3	B x N
10. Q x B	O—O!

Very aggressive — and therefore unexpected from a man who needs the draw! Black is prepared to see his P position in ruins (K4, QB2, QB3, QR4) in the belief that piece play along the QN-file and the black centre squares will be full compensation. Of course, he will have to "invent" something all the time, but that is not a bad thing in the circumstances: against a strong opponent nothing is less calculated to obtain a draw than a game without any initiative (a lesson I finally learnt against Pachman at the Marianske Lazne zonal tournament in 1951).

11. B x N	P x B
12. N—N3	B—K2
13. B—K3	Q—N1!

Threatening both Q—N5 and Q—N4—B5. Thus White at once protects his KP.

14. KR—K1	P—QR4
15. P—QR4	R—Q1
16. Q—B5	N—Q2

Not merely in order to protect the KP, but to play the N via B1 to K3 whence it will threaten both N—Q5 and P—QB4—B5.

17. QR—Q1	P—N3

18. Q—N4	N—B1
19. R x R	B x R
20. P—KB4!	

If Black succeeds in playing the N to K3 and the Q, say, to N5, he will have the advantage. On the other hand, his K is now almost completely denuded of defensive units, so obviously White must attack. The following part of the game is most difficult and as a result both players run short of time.

20. ...,	P x P
21. Q x P	N—K3
22. Q—K5	B—K2

Black finds the time to get his pieces back to the defence, for if now 23. N—Q4, he has the resource, 23. ..., QxP!; while 23. NxP?, can be answered with 23. ..., Q—N5.

23. R—KB1!	B—Q3

Forcing the Q off the 5th rank and thus relieving the pressure on the QRP.

24. Q—B6	Q—KB1
25. N—Q4	

25. B—R6, QxB!; 26. QxBPch, K—R1; 27. QxN, Q—K6ch; 28. K—R1, Q—N6; 29. Q—B6ch, K—N1; 30. K—N1!, Q—K6ch; 31. Q—B2, QxKP; gives White nothing.

25. ...,	Q—N2!

The point of the defensive build-up. If now 26. NxN, QxQ; 27. RxQ, PxN; 28. RxKP?, K—B2; would win the exchange. Or 26. NxP, QxQ; 27. RxQ, R—R3; 28. N—N8 (28. N—

Q4?, B—K4!), R—R1; 29. N—B6 (29. N—Q7?, R—Q1!), with repetition of moves. Or 26. QxQch, KxQ; 27. NxP, R—R3; 28. N—Q4 (or 28. N—N8, R—R1; 29. N—Q7, R—Q1; 30. N—B6, B—K4), N—B4!; and Black regains his pawn.

26. Q—B2

And yet White should have tried 26. NxN, QxQ; 27. RxQ, PxN; and now perhaps 28. B—R6, with some initiative, for the text gives him nothing. Certainly the R + B ending was White's best chance.

26. ...,	**R—KB1**
27. N x P	**Q x P**

28. N x P

Allowing an immediate forced draw, but I doubt whether White had any advantage left at this stage.

28. ...,	**Q—K4!**

Threatening mate and N — White's reply is forced.

29. Q—Q2	**Q—R7 ch**
30. K—B2	**Q—N6 ch!**
31. K—N1	

and draw by perpetual check. Since a draw was as good as a win, there was no point in experimenting with 30. ..., B—N6ch; 31. K—B3, P—KB4; 32. P—K5!, BxP; 33. Q—Q5!, which is very unclear.

Game No. 40.

When you have adopted an unusual build-up, either from choice or under compulsion, you cannot then pretend that nothing has happened and treat a climb up a steep cliff like a stroll along the sandy beach. Sharp situations demand sharp action. The following game, played in the Dublin Whitsun week-end tournament of 1966, is a striking example.

Black: K. O'Riordan.

Pirc Defence.

1. P—K4	P—Q3
2. P—Q4	N—KB3
3. N—QB3	P—KN3
4. B—KN5	B—N2
5. Q—Q2	

In this line of play White always does well not to give Black a chance of going into some line of the King's Indian; in other words, not to waste time on P—QB4 which (a) does not develop a piece and (b) lengthens the diagonal of the black KB.

5. ...,	QN—Q2
6. N—B3	P—B4
7. B—QB4	P x P
8. N x P	

Now the game is a Sicilian Dragon in which Black has played the inferior move, QN—Q2, instead of N—QB3. As Black plays, his "dragon" will be killed before he can do any harm.

8. ...,	P—QR3
9. B—N3	P—N4

10. P—B3	B—N2
11. B—R6	B x B
12. Q x B	R—KN1
13. N—Q5?	

There is no hurry for this — White should first render Black's freeing manoeuvre of the next few moves innocuous by playing P—KR4!

13. ...,	B x N
14. P x B	N—B4
15. O—O—O	N x B ch
16. N x N	P—N4!

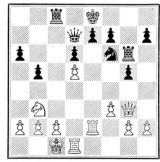

Position after White's 20th move.

88

17. KR—K1	R—N3
18. Q—R3	Q—Q2
19. Q—N3	R—B1
20. R—K2	

See diagram on previous page.

This is the position referred to in the introduction. Black should now put the question to the QP: 20. . . . , Q—B4! Possibly he overlooked that White cannot answer 21. QxQP?, because of 21. . . . , RxPch.

Getting rid of the cramping QP is a necessity if Black wants to survive. This does not mean that he would have had the superior game after 20. . . . , Q—B4; 21. Q—B2!, NxP; 22. Q—R7!, and now (a) 22. . . . , Q—B5 ch; 23. K—N1, Q—B5; 24. QxP (threatening mate on B8, so that Black has no time for 24. . . . , QxR), N—N5; 25. Q—N7, R—K3; 26. R(2)—Q2, with chances for both sides. Or (b) 22. . . . , R—K3; 23. R(2)—Q2! (not 23. N—Q4?, RxR; 24. NxQ, R(1)xP ch and wins), N—K6; 24. N—Q4, Q—Q4; again with a full game.

Instead of grasping this one chance of getting out from under, he hits on the unfortunate idea of bringing his N from the good square KB3 to the bad square KB5.

20. . . . ,	N—R4?
21. Q—B2	N—B5
22. R—K4	R—B5
23. P—N3	R x R
24. P x R	N—R6
25. Q—N6	

A terrible change has come over the scene. The white QP, far from vulnerable, has received pawn support, all black pieces are displaced, and all white pieces at their maximum efficiency.

25. . . . ,	Q—B1
26. N—R5	

Of course not 26. N—Q4?, N—B7! In order to threaten this manoeuvre, Black has now to waste a fatal move.

26. . . . ,	R—B3
27. N—B6	N—B7
28. Q—R7	K—B1
29. Q x P ch	K—N2
30. R—K1	N—N5
31. P—KR4!	P—R3
32. P x P	P x P
33. N—Q4	N—R3
34. N—K6 ch	K—N3
35. R—R1	R x N

The curse of the R-file! If 35. . . . , PxN; 36. RxNch, followed by 37. QxRch, and 38. PxP. If 35. . . . , N—N1; 36. N—B8ch, K—N2; 37. R—R7 mate. If 35. . . . , Q—KR1; 36. P—K5!, PxP; 37. N—B8ch, K—N2; 38. N—Q7, R—N3; 39. NxP, R—KB3; 40. N—N4, R—KN3; 41. NxN, RxN; 42. QxNPch.

36. P x R	Q x P
37. Q—B8!	K—R2

Now Black can only shuffle his Q from K3 to KB3 and back, while White prepares the liquidation of all the pieces, leaving a simple pawn ending.

38. P—KN4	Q—KB3
39. K—N1	P—R4
40. P—R3	P—N5
41. P x P	P x P
42. P—N3	Q—K3
43. R x N ch	**Resigns**

After the double exchange White plays P—B3, either queening the NP or winning all the pawns.

Game No. 41.

"Any fool can sacrifice a piece, but it takes a smart chap to sacrifice a pawn," Tartakower must have said somewhere or other ; or if he didn't he merely forgot to do so. There is certainly nothing like a pawn sacrifice to change the fundamentals of a position, as in the following game from the Irish Championship at Belfast 1966.

Black: M. O'Leary.
French Defence (in effect).

1. P—K4	P—QB4
2. P—QB3	P—K3
3. P—Q4	P—Q4
4. P—K5	N—QB3

The normal position of the French Advance variation has now been reached. Personally, I prefer Wade's 4. . . . , Q—N3 (see game No. 24).

5. N—B3	P x P(?)
6. P x P	Q—N3
7. N—B3	B—N5(?)
8. B—Q3	B—Q2
9. B—K3	KN—K2
10. O—O	B x N
11. P x B	N—R4

Black's play, while unorthodox, is not without point: a forepost on QB5 and play on the half-open file; but as I have mentioned before in other openings (the Alapin Sicilian and the Advance variation of the Caro-Kann) this never compensates fully for the weakness on the black squares.

12. Q—K2	R—QB1
13. QR—N1	Q—B2
14. B—Q2	

With the idea of luring the N to QB5 at once and then using its presence there for a *petite combinaison*.

14. . . . ,	N—B5
15. B—N5	P—KR3?

It is immaterial that the black King is forced to move since artificial castling can be effected without difficulty, but Black should have safeguarded his QNP by 15. . . . , P—QN3!

16. B x KN!	K x B
17. B x N	P x B

For now he cannot play the otherwise desirable 17. . . . , QxB; because of 18. QxQ, RxQ; 19. RxP, P—QR4; 20. N—Q2!, RxBP; 21. N—N3, P—R5; 22. N—B5, R—Q1; 23. R—R7, R—QR6; 24. R—N1, RxP; 25. P—R3, K—K1; 26. R(1)—N7, and wins.

18. P—Q5!

This pawn sacrifice is the point of White's play: the N will get the square Q4, the KB is free to advance for a K-side attack, and the black position in the centre is blocked. Whether the sacrifice should have led to a forced win, however, is doubtful.

18. . . . ,	P x P
19. N—Q4	KR—K1
20. P—B4	K—B1
21. QR—K1	P—KN3
22. Q—K3	K—N2?

Black under-estimates the danger, for this instinctive "protection" of the KRP loses out of hand. 22. . . . , B—B4; would lose the exchange because of 23. N—N5, followed by N—Q6, but 22. . . . , Q—N3!; would have guarded QN4, protected KR3 indirectly and gained a move because of the pin on the long diagonal. White intended to reply 23. K—R1, and now:

(a) 23. . . . , K—N2?; 24. P—N4!, BxP; 25. R—KN1, followed by 26. P—B5, and should win.

(b) 23. . . . , B—B4; 24. NxB, PxN; 25. Q—R3, Q—K3; 26. Q—R4, with the deadly threat of 27. P—N4.

(c) 23. . . . , P—KR4! This is the critical variation, in which White will have to extend the stakes to three pawns without, however, being sure of the outcome: 24. P—B5!, PxP! (if 24. . . . , BxP; 25. Q—R6ch, K—N1; 26. NxB, PxN; 27. QxP, Q—N3; 28. Q—

Q1!, seems the simplest way of securing an advantage: the extra black pawn is meaningless in view of the exposed position of his King); 25. P—K6!, BxP! (25. ..., PxP?; 26. Q—R6ch, K—K2; 27. NxPch, K—Q1; 28. Q—B6ch, K—B2; 29. Q—K5ch, K—Q1; 30. N—Q6, is clearly hopeless); 26. Q—R6ch, K—K2; and if then either 27. NxPch, or 27. RxP, Black answers 27. ..., K—Q2; and has fair chances of survival. In fact, I have stared at this position for days without finding anything definite—perhaps one of my readers will be more successful.

23. P—B5   P x P

24. R x P!   Q—N3

If 24. ..., BxR; 25. NxBch, followed by either 26. Q—N3ch, or 26. QxRPch, according to Black's reply.

25. R—B6	**R—B3**
26. Q x P ch	**K—N1**
27. Q—N5 ch	**K—B1**
28. R x P ch!	**K x R**
29. R—B1 ch	**Resigns**

It is unfortunate that Black, as a result of his weak 22nd move, did not really test the correctness of White's conception (impossible to calculate to the end); even so, the typical black-square attack (by move 25 ALL white pieces are on black squares) is the logical result of White's previous play.

Game No. 42.

One may have a lost game and yet have plenty of counter-play (compare, e.g. the games against Najdorf and Czerniak). What is far worse — at least to me — is having the inferior position without any hope of breathing life into it. To put back hope into such a hopeless fight needs a bit of co-operation from the opponent, as e.g. in the following game from the Irish Championship at Belfast 1966. The moral is: where there is no hope, don't give up — hope!

Black: E. Whiteside.
Niemzovich Defence.

1. P—K4	**N—QB3**
2. P—Q4	**P—K4**

The true "Niemzovich" continues with 2. ..., P—Q4; which in my early days I occasionally played myself. The text took me by surprise — and my next moves show it!

3. P—Q5

Best is probably 3. PxP, NxP; 4. N—KB3, whereas 3. N—KB3 at once is a transposition to the Scotch Game which (a) does not promise White much and (b) is virgin territory to me. The text is certainly no better and, with White's next planned at this stage, decidedly worse.

3. ...,	**QN—K2**
4. P—KB4?	**P x P!**

With this and his next few moves Black will get square K4 for his pieces.

5. B x P	**N—N3**
6. B—N3	**B—B4**
7. KN—B3	**P—Q3**
8. N—B3	**P—QR3!**

Providing a retreat for the Bishop.

9. B—Q3	**N—B3**
10. Q—K2	**O—O**
11. O—O—O	**N—N5!**
12. P—KR3	**N(5)—K4**
13. N x N	**N x N**
14. B x N	**Q—N4 ch!**
15. K—N1	**Q x B**

White has "developed" without much purpose — Black has pointedly played for the control of the black squares, leaving White with a backward pawn on an open file and the inferior Bishop as well.

16. QR—KB1	**B—Q2**
17. N—Q1	**P—QN4**

91

| 18. N—B2 | B x N |
| 19. R x B | QR—N1 |

Black has retained his positional advantage and now is ready to throw his Q-side pawns into the attack. If White tries to stem the attack by an exchange of Queens, he will be left with a lifeless position and the horrible target on K4. I looked at the melancholy position for a long time and decided I had to shift that ugly fat woman on my K5 at any cost. Did I have the time? Perhaps.

20. KR—KB1	P—QR4
21. R—B4!	P—R5
22. Q—KB3	

Around this time my opponent told Littleton that he had a completely won game. "You had better be careful," said Littleton, "you are playing the dirtiest player in Ireland".

| 22. . . . , | P—R6? |

Black disregards one of the basic principles of chess, which Purdy has christened "reserving the greater opion". Thus 22. . . . , P—KB3!; which will be necessary anyway, should have been played first and the option of continuing the attack with either P—R6 or P—N5 preserved. But Black dreams of a R sacrifice on QR7 to crown his work, sees no danger and succumbs before the R ever has a chance to get to his destination.

23. P x P	P—KB3
24. R—R4	R—R1
25. R—R5!	

At last — getting this R into a respectable attacking position seemed to take ages. Naturally Black should have stopped the whole business with 22. . . . , P—KB3!; 23. R—R4, P—N3!

See diagram opposite.

| 25. . . . , | P—N4 |

If, e.g. 25. . . . , Q—B6; 26. P—K5! wins at once, while 25. . . . , P—KB4; allows 26. PxP, RxRP; 27. P—B6!

Black's most interesting defensive try was 25. . . . , Q—Q5; 26. P—K5,

Position after White's 25th move.

P—KB4! (not 26. . . . , P—N3?; 27. RxP!, PxP; 28. R—B7); 27. P—K6, RxP; 28. Q—B4, QxQ; 29. RxQ, P—N3; 30. PxB!, PxR; 31. RxP! and White has the advantage.

| 26. R—R6! | R x P |

26. . . . , K—N2; is answered with 27. Q—R5 — miraculously each step of White's freeing manoeuvre is achieved with tempo.

27. R x KBP	R x R
28. Q x R	Q x Q
29. R x Q	K—N2
30. R—B2	B—K1?

Disconcerted by the turn of events, Black allows White to make his Bishop "good" at once. The B should have been kept on Q2 and the R played back.

| 31. K—N2 | R—R1 |
| 32. P—K5! | |

Dissolving the white-squared roadblock, which constituted Black's last drawing chance.

32. . . . ,	P x P
33. R—B5	B—N3
34. R x KP	B x B
35. P x B	K—B3
36. R—K6 ch	K—B2
37. R—QB6	R—R2
38. K—N3	K—K2
39. R—KR6	K—Q2
40. P—Q6!	R—R3
41. R x P ch	Resigns

The QP had a charmed life.

Game No. 43.

The rarely-seen opening line employed in the following game (first recommended by "Niemzovich the Bizarre" and later highly praised by the ultrasound Klaus Junge!) is the only line with which I have never yet lost a game — this despite the fact that I have used it at least twenty times, and against such formidable opposition as Unzicker (see game No. 47), Kupper, Levy (Scotland), Safvat (Iran), in addition to many local experts as well as my opponent in the present game, played in the first round of the Habana International Team Tournament 1966.

White: R. Letelier.
French Defence.

1. P—Q4	P—K3
2. P—K4	P—Q4
3. N—QB3	N—KB3
4. B—N5	B—K2
5. P—K5	N—N1

This is the line referred to. One of its advantages is that it renders the Alekhine-Chatard Gambit (6. P—KR4) extremely doubtful — after 6. ..., BxB!; 7. PxB, QxP; 8. N—R3, Q—K2; 9. Q—N4, P—KB4!; or 9. N—B4, P—KN3; Black can develop his QN via Q2 and KB1 and achieve an early O—O—O — in the normal lines the KN blocks square Q2. Strangely enough, Keres, the great expert on the French, does not even mention the acceptance of the gambit in his book!

6. B—K3	P—QN3
7. N—B3(!)	

This natural developing move is a sort of innovation. In the more usual build-up White continues with Q—N4 and P—KR4, which merely forces Black to make the moves he wants to play in any case, viz. P—KN3 and P—KR4.

7. ...,	B—R3
8. B x B	N x B
9. Q—K2	N—N1
10. O—O	Q—Q2
11. KR—K1	

White has an overwhelming lead in development but nothing to bite at and no chance of effectively opening the game. Meanwhile Black, rid of his problem child, the QB, has sufficient space behind the pawn wall to disentangle his pieces.

11. ...,	N—QB3
12. N—N1	B—Q1

Black is in no hurry to castle — first the pieces must be brought out, especially a Knight to keep an eye on square Q4 in case White tries to open the position by P—QB4. It is interesting to compare the similar manoeuvring (with different pieces, because the white Q is on the K-side) in the game against Unzicker (game No. 47).

13. QN—Q2	KN—K2

Now White has developed "three" Knights, Black "four" — no wonder Black wins!

14. P—B3	N—B4
15. B—N5	B x B
16. N x B	P—KR3
17. N—R3	O—O—O
18. Q—R6 ch	K—N1
19. P—QN4?	

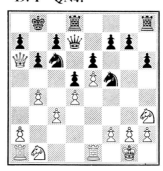

This move allows a surprising combination, which is easy to see afterwards. It is based on the off-side posi-

93

tion of the white KN. If 19. P—QR4 instead, Black would have been ready to attack the centre by 19. ..., P—KB3.

19. ...,	**N(4) x QP!**
20. P—N5	

Attempting a refutation. If 20. PxN, NxNP; 21. Q—K2, N—B7; and after capturing one of the Rooks, Black plays R—QB1 and is at last ready for P—QB4, after which R and two central pawns should be stronger than two Knights.

20. ...,	**N—B7**
21. Q—R4	**N(3)—N5!**
22. P x N	

Possibly White had planned 22. KR—B1, so as to answer 22. ..., NxR; with 23. QxN!, P—Q5; 24. P—B4, P—Q6; 25. RxN, but Black would play the immediate 22. ..., P—Q5; and obtain better chances than in the game.

22. ...,	**N x QR**
23. R x N	**P—Q5**
24. Q—N3	**Q x P**
25. N—QB4	**P—Q6**

Hereabouts Eddie Price, of the South African team, remarked to me that the advance of the QP acted like a bore, the concentrated force behind the pawn expanding as the pawn marched on.

26. P—R4	**Q—Q4**
27. R—Q1	**P—KN4**
28. P—B3	

Reminding Black that he has an extra piece to bear on the QP, by N—B2. Thus Black has to find a way of over-protecting this pawn.

28. ...,	**Q—B3!**

Which he achieves by removing one guard. If now 29. RxP, RxR; 30. QxR, QxRP; and Black has nothing to worry about. White, however, consistently plays for the gain, not the exchange, of this pawn.

29. N—B2	**R—Q5**
30. N—K3	**P—Q7**

31. N—K4	**R(1)—Q1**
32. P—N5	**Q—Q2**

Of course not 32. ..., Q—B8?; 33. NxQP!

33. Q—N2!

Most exciting complications would have followed the alternative, 33. Q—B2, viz. 33. ..., R—Q6; 34. N—B4, Q—Q5ch; 35. K—B1, P—N5!; 36. N—N2, R—K6; and now:

(a) 37. RxP, R—K8ch!; 38. KxR, Q—N8ch; 39. K—K2, QxPch; 40. N—B2, PxPch; 41. K—K3, Q—N4ch; 42. KxP, RxR and wins. 40. K—K1! would, in this line, force Black to take the draw, of course.

(b) 37. NxP?, R—B6!; 38. Q—K4, PxP; 39. PxP, QxQ; 40. PxQ, R—B7! and wins. Or 38. Q—N1, Q—KB5; 39. N—N3 (39. N—K4, RxRch; 40. NxR, R—B8; 41. Q—N3, QxRP and wins), RxRch; 40. QxR, QxRP and White has no defence. If in this line 39. P—N3, Q—K6; 40. N(N)—B4, RxN(B5); 41. NxR, QxPch; 42. K—K1, Q—B6ch; 43. N—Q2, Q—K6ch and wins, or 43. R—Q2, R—Q5 and wins.

(c) 37. QxP!, and now not 37. ..., RxN? (which I gave in the East German tournament book and would have played) because of 38. Q—QB2!, PxP; 39. PxP!, and White wins (but not immediately 39. RxQ, PxPch; 40. KxP, R(5)x R; 41. N—B4, R(1)—Q4; and whatever winning chances there are would be with Black). Better is 37. ..., QxQ; 38. RxR, RxR; 39. NxR, PxP; 40. NxP, R—N6; and Black wins the QRP and will quickly establish a phalanx of passed pawns on the Q-side.

If White diverges earlier and tries 34. N—B1 (instead of 34. N—B4), there would follow 34. ..., Q—Q5ch; 35. N—B2, R—B6; and now either

94

36. Q—N2, R—B8!; retaining the QP, or 36. QxP, QxQ; 37. RxQ, RxR; 38. NxR, R—B8ch; 39. N—B1, R—R8; and Black will again have threatening passed pawns in an even better position.

With the text White keeps control of square Q4 and now threatens to attack the QP a fourth time. But the very existence of such complicated alternatives, some of which both partner had to look into, caused White to run exceedingly short of time, with disastrous consequences just prior to the adjournment.

| 33. ..., | R x N |

Cutting the Gordian knot and bringing about an ending with three pawns for the Knight.

34. P x R	Q—Q6
35. N—B1	Q x KP
36. R x P	R x R
37. N x R	Q x RP
38. P—R3	Q—Q8 ch

A bit of psychological chess: Black played this move *a tempo*, without giving the opponent any time for thought: if a player in extreme time pressure opens a hole for his King, it can be expected that he will walk into it. Objectively, the immediate 38. ..., K—N2 ; followed by P—R3, may well have been better.

39. K—R2?

With his flag trembling on the brink, he is caught in a virtual *zugzwang*. 39. K—B2!, should have been played.

| 39. ..., | Q—K7! |

Pinning the N and attacking both KP and NP. White is now virtually forced to give a fourth pawn, and that is too much.

| 40. Q—Q4 | Q x NP |
| 41. Q—Q8 ch | K—N2 |

42. Q—B6	Q—N5
43. N—B3	Q—B5 ch
44. K—N1	Q x Q?

A blemish typical of team play. As the Chileans told us afterwards, on 44. ..., P—QR4! Letelier would have resigned at once; after 45. QxRP, his pieces would be strangely helpless against the advance of the QRP, e.g. 45. QxRP, Q—B8ch! ; 46. K—R2, P—R5; 47. Q—B8, P—R6; 48. Q—N4, P—R7. I chose the text because the Irish team had analysed a clear win in the N ending even before I had finished my dinner.

45. P x Q	P—QR4
46. N—K5	P—R5
47. N x P	K—B1!

This is the joke that ensures the win. If now 48. NxNP, K—Q2; 49. P—B7, K—K2; 50. NxP, KxP; 51. NxP, P—R6. If White refrains from capturing the fourth pawn it makes no difference.

48. N—Q6 ch	K—Q2
49. N—N5	P—B3
50. N—Q4	P—R6
51. P—B7	P—R7
52. P—B8(N) ch	

Since the Q ending after 52. P—B8 (Q), would be hopeless anyway, White has his bit of fun to wind up with, incidentally "developing" his fourth N after all. Unfortunately it is too late now.

52. ...,	K—K1
53. N—N3	K x N
54. K—B2	K—K2
55. K—K3	K—Q3
56. K—Q4	P—B4 ch
57. K—B3	K—K4
Resigns	

The black K eats up the remaining pawns.

Game No. 44.

To hold an inferior position against one of the foremost players of the age, who is out for the kill, is a thrill not often enjoyed by a common and garden player, and I am pleased it came my way in the preliminaries of the Habana team tournament. Of course, there are always two sides to such a story, and I wonder how much this game meant to Larsen. It reminds me of the occasion when Kenneth Kirby bought innumerable copies of the picture showing him in play against Botvinnik at the Tel Aviv team tournament and Pines, the former Rhodesian champion and now resident in Israel, asked him with an innocent smile how many copies he thought Botvinnik would order of this picture!

Black: B. Larsen.
Sicilian Defence.

1.	P—K4	P—QB4
2.	P—QB3	N—KB3
3.	P—K5	N—Q4
4.	N—B3	N—QB3
5.	N—R3	P—KN3
6.	P—KN3	B—N2
7.	B—N2	O—O
8.	O—O	P—Q3
9.	P x P	Q x P
10.	P—Q4	P x P
11.	N—QN5	Q—B4
12.	N(5) x QP	R—Q1!

Larsen has chosen the strongest line against White's pet variation. I was a little surprised at his going into this line, as I had reached the identical position against Portisch (Madrid 1960), where I had blithely continued 13. NxN, PxN; 14. Q—R4, R—N1; 15. N—Q4, B—Q2; 16. N—N3, Q—N3; 17. Q—R4, and the game soon fizzled out into a draw. Knowing how carefully Larsen is apt to prepare his openings, I had a closer look at this point and came to the conclusion that the isolation of Black's QBP could not possibly profit White's game in view of the open QN-file. I have not discussed the position with Larsen, but feel he might have substituted the subtle prophylactic move, 14. ..., B—B3!; for Portisch's 14th. If then 15. B—N5, R—N1!; is so much stronger with the NP immediately under fire: 16. BxB, NxB; 17. Q—B2, is immediately refuted by 17. ..., B—B4!; if 16.

BxB, NxB; 17. N—Q4, R—Q3!; which cannot be answered with 18. NxP (or 18. BxP, P—K4), B—Q2; 19. QxP, QxQ; 20. NxQ, R—R3; and Black wins a piece; and if 16. BxB, NxB; 17. P—N3, N—K5; when 18. P—B4, is not playable because of 18. ..., R—N5; 19. Q—R3, RxBP!

Whatever the merits or otherwise of this position, this is a most instructive example of how differently one appraises positions at different times, for back in 1960 the move 13. NxN, had seemed absolutely natural to me.

13.	Q—R4	N—N3

With 13. ..., NxN; 14. PxN! (14. NxN?, N—N3; 15. Q—N5?, BxN;) Black could have rendered White's efforts to recapture on Q4 with a piece futile. But after 14. ..., Q—N5; 15. Q—N3!, White would get excellent play in exchange for his ruined pawn position, e.g. 15. ..., B—K3; 16. B—Q2, QxQ; 17. PxQ, N—N3; 18. R—R3! After the text it is Black who gets the piece play and White's only consolation is that he has no static pawn weaknesses.

14.	Q—N5	Q x Q
15.	N x Q	P—K4
16.	B—N5	P—B3
17.	B—B1!	

This manoeuvre has served to take the heat off the QB3—QN2 weakness; supplemented by the further artificial regrouping of the next four moves it succeeds in shaking off the pressure to some extent.

17. ...,	B—B4
18. N—R3	N—R5
19. R—K1	R—Q2
20. B—B1	QR—Q1
21. B—QN5	N—B4
22. B—K3	N—Q6

This is the ultimate price White has to pay for keeping his pawn position intact: the pair of Bishops. It certainly was the least evil.

23. B x N	B x B
24. QR—B1	P—KR3
25. KR—Q1	P—B4
26. N—K1	

So far the only good moves White has been allowed to make have been re-developing moves to the back rank — yet his play has not been without sting. Larsen's reply in the text was afterwards criticized by him because of the tactical chance it gives. Since, however, 26. ..., B—K7; 27. RxR, RxR; 28. P—B3!, followed by 29. K—B2, also does not seem to leave Black with much; he had to burn his boats and dig himself in on Q6 with P—K5. At least, if this is not good enough, nothing else is.

26. ...,	B—R3
27. R x R	R x R
28. P—QN4!	

This surprising thrust cannot be countered with 28. ..., P—QN4; because of 29. P—QB4! It completely frees White's game.

28. ...,	B—B1

39. N(1)—B2	B—Q6
30. P—N5	N—K2

Stopping 31. BxP, because of 31. ..., N—Q4; with multiple threats, yet after White's reply the black pieces get into each other's way. During the game I was far more worried about 30. ..., N—Q1; 31. BxP, N—K3; which is not easy to assess. I certainly would have grabbed the pawn and hoped for the best.

31. P—QB4!	N—B1
32. P—B5	P—R3
33. P x P	B x RP
34. N—N4	B—K7

The only vague threat now is B—B6 with mating threats if the white R has to go on business trips abroad. But the active white pieces manage to scotch this threat easily enough.

35. N—B4	B—N2
36. P—B6	P x P
37. N x BP	P—K5
38. N(4)—K5	R—Q3
39. N—Q4!	

With my flag trembling.

39. ...,	B—R3
40. P—B4	N—K2
41. N—N3!	

Over this, my sealed move, I took over half an hour. It is easily the best, its principal merit being that it makes QB5 available for either B or N and thus opposes the threat of 41. ..., N—Q4. During the adjournment the Irish team looked at 41. ..., N—Q4; 42. B—B5, R—K3; 43. N—Q4, RxN; 44. PxR, BxP; but the white pieces are far too active for the black pawns to become a serious threat and White might well win. Larsen stops B—B5 but allows a different simplification.

41. ...,	R—Q4
42. N—B6	N x N

Otherwise White would play 43. N—N4.

43. R x N	B—K7!

Not 43. ..., R—Q8ch; 44. K—B2,

R—B8ch; 45. K—N2. Nor can Black play passively because White would simply take the NP. After the text this would be no good because of 44. ..., R—Q8ch; 45. K—B2, B—R4!; 46. R—QB6, R—KR8.

44. R—B8 ch   K—B2
45. R—B7 ch   K—N1
46. R—B8 ch

and drawn by repetition of moves. It would not help Black to play the K to R2, for after R—B7 White would threaten B—Q4.

Some years later, at Castlebar, Brinck Claussen told me that Larsen expected to win this game and felt robbed somehow. A bit of larseny, so to speak.

Game No. 45.

Played in the Dublin league matches 1967, the following game bears a certain resemblance to my previous game against the same opponent (see No. 38): the play with Rooks and Knights, the ineffectiveness of the exchange of Queens in killing combinational turns, etc. Yet in essentials the games are entirely different; whereas No. 38 was a "technically" won game in which the combinations led to a demonstrable win, the present encounter was a "real game of chess" — with everything in flux and the outcome in the balance in every combinational variation, prior to Black's error on move 21.

Black: E. A. Keogh.
French Defence.

1. P—K4	P—K3	9. P—N6?!	P—B4
2. P—Q4	P—Q4	10. Q—N3	P—R3
3. N—QB3	N—KB3	11. N—B3	
4. B—N5	B—K2		
5. P—K5	KN—Q2		
6. P—KR4	P—QR3		
7. Q—N4	B x B(?!)		

A peculiar continuation instead of the theoretical moves 7. ..., K—B1; or 7. ..., P—KB4. At first glance one is inclined to say: "if Black is prepared to open the KR-file, he might at least have taken the pawn for his pains". Yet the matter is not quite so simple: having prevented N—QN5, Black stands ready to counter the white K-side attack by assaulting the centre pawns, and if White wants to exploit the chances offered as a result of Black's last move, he will have to forgo safeguarding his vital KP by means of P—KB4. This precarious balance between King-side attack and centre attack is the theme of the coming middle game.

8. P x P   P—QB4

Not only protecting the QP but also threatening N—KN5. Black is thus virtually forced to castle, after which he must be on the alert against an eventual RxRP all the time.

11. ...,	0—0!
12. Q—B4	N—QB3
13. 0—0—0	P x P
14. KN x P	N x N

Here the problem arises for the first time: could Black have played 14. ..., N(2)xP; 15. NxN, NxN? White would answer 16. B—B4, and threaten a sacrifice on Q5 — note that Black can neither get the King off the dangerous diagonal by 16. ..., K—R1?; because of 17. RxPch, nor obstruct the second rank by 16. ..., N—K2; again because of 17. RxRP!

Faulty would be the "elegant" 16. NxP?!, which I suggested in my notes shortly after the game. Black would answer 16. ..., PxN!; 17. RxQP, Q—N4!; 18. QxQ, PxQ; 19. B—B4 (if 19. R—Q7, P—N4!; with the threat

98

of an early R—B3), B—K3! (but not now 19. ..., P—N4?; 20. R—Q8 dis ch, PxB; 21. R—R8ch, KxR; and the sole remaining Rook gives mate). In the resultant position White does not get enough for his piece, for if then 20. R—Q7, BxB; 21. R—R7, B—B2!; and if 20. R—K1, N—R4! (only!).

15. R x N   Q—N4!

Here the problem arises for the second time: would White get enough for his pawn after 15. Q—B2? — 16. RxQP?, PxR; 17. NxP, QxKP; 18. N—K7ch, QxN; 19. B—B4ch, R—B2; would not work, but after 16. NxP!, PxN; 17. RxQP, P—N4! (not 17. ..., N—N3; 18. R—Q6, B—Q2; 19. RxN!, QxR; 20. RxP!, PxR; 21. QxRP, R—B2; 22. PxRch, and wins the Queen); 18. Q—Q4, would give White a very strong game with two pawns for the piece; he would also at last have the possibility of supporting the KP by P—KB4. The text looks much sounder.

16. Q x Q   P x Q
17. R x P!

This unexpected move (temporarily winning a pawn and protecting the KP once again) shows that the exchange of Queens was not the end of the combinational turns. Actually, the R can be taken: after 17. ..., PxR; 18. NxP, R—Q1!; 19. N—B7 (not the tempting 19. N—K7ch, K—B1; 20. NxP, K—K1!), NxP; 20. NxR, B—K3; 21. N—B7, BxP!; 22. P—QN3, R—

QB1; 23. N—Q5, R—B4; 24. N—K7ch, K—B1; 25. NxP, BxP! (but not 25. ..., NxP?; 26. N—Q4, R—Q4; 27. P—QB3!, and wins the B); 26. R—R 8ch, B—N1; 27. N—Q4, R—B1! (not 27. ..., NxP?; 28. N—K6ch, and wins; 28. N—K6ch, K—K2; 29. NxP (5), the ending offers about even chances. But it was not easy to foresee the many twists and turns of this passage, and Black reasons correctly that the white pawns on K5 and N6 are not likely to grow stronger as time goes by.

17. ...,   R—K1
18. R—Q6

Now White can no longer maintain the generous offer.

18. ...,   N x P
19. B—K2   P—N4

On 19. ..., P—N5 (to stop an eventual B—R5); Keogh did not like the prospects of 20. P—B3 — too early an opening of lines cannot benefit his King in his present state of undress.

20. R—K1

The KNP cannot be held; if 20. B—R5 at once, 20. ..., N—B5; 21. R—B6, B—N2; 22. R—B7, BxP; 23. R—N1, B—Q4; 24. RxP, the black pieces co-operate well and the P on N6 remains a liability.

20. ...,   N x P
21. B—R5   K—B2?

At last Black falters. Correct was the unnatural-looking 21. ..., K—R2! If then 22. R—R1, R—R2!; White has nothing. If 22. N—Q5, R—R2; and White has to wind up with 23. N—N6, as in the game, but about two moves behind. After the text Black will have *two* pieces in the fatal pin of the B, and this makes all the difference.

22. N—Q5!   R—R1
23. N—N6   R—QN1
24. B x N ch

Objectively, a still more favourable ending was to be had with 24. N—Q7!

But with both sides now very short of time, Black might have played *va banque* with 24. ..., RxB!? ; 25. NxR, P—K4; giving up exchange and pawn for the sake of his K-side pawns — with this type of material anything may happen in time trouble. The denouement chosen leaves Black no swindling chances of any sort.

24. ...,	K x B
25. N x B	R(R) x N
26. R(6) x P ch	K—R2
27. R(1)—K5	R—B5
28. R x BP	R(1)—QB1
29. R—K2	K—N3
30. R(5)—K5	R(1)—B3
31. R—K6 ch	K—B2

32. R x R	R x R
33. P—QB3	K—B3
34. P—KN4	R—Q3
35. K—B2	K—B2

This sly move threatens to regain the pawn, but unfortunately for Black material has become immaterial: the QBP marches through. There followed: 36. P—N3, R—KB3; 37. P—QB4, PxP; 38. PxP, R—B5; 39. K—Q3, RxNP; 40. P—B5, R—KR5; 41. P—B6, R—R3; 42. R—B2, R—R1; 43. K—Q4, K—K3; 44. K—B5, K—K2; 45. K—N6, R—N1ch; 46. K—R7, Resigns.

This is the most interesting game I have played against an Irish player.

Game No. 46.

Scientific research into specific types of end-games is older than tournament chess. The findings of Philidor in the ending of R + B vs. R stand unsurpassed to this very day. Other important research that comes to my mind is that by Troitsky on the ending of two N's vs. P, that by Dr. Tarrasch on the ending of Bishops of opposite colours with one side having two connected passed pawns, or that by Chéron on the ending of R vs. B with one facing RP each.

The ending reached in the following game, played at the Irish Championship at Cork 1967, is also of a type on which a great deal of detailed investigation by very great masters has been lavished. It has been known for long that the specific ending of Q + NP vs. Q presents problems absent from other Q + P vs. Q endings, and detailed analysis and discussion of these problems has been published by Keres and Botvinnik in connection with two games of Botvinnik's, against Ravinsky and Minev. When the present game was published in the *British Chess Magazine* (November 1967), it drew, among other correspondence, an admirably erudite letter from A. J. Roycroft, the well-known end-game expert and study composer, in which he gave a thumbnail sketch of the research conducted into this ending, which culminated in a special competition run by *Shakmaty vs. USSR* in 1955 and evaluated by Awerbakh in the June and July 1959 issues of *Shakmatny Bulletin*.

The course and conduct of the ending reached in the present game more or less confirm previous findings. It is always more interesting to fly in the face of established precedent and discover something new, but in the case of so rare an ending even the confirmation of previously-known principles and techniques cannot be said to be wholly devoid of value.

Black: N. J. Patterson.
French Defence (in effect).

1. P—K4	P—QB4
2. P—QB3	P—K3

4. P—K5	N—K2
5. N—B3	QN—B3
6. B—K3?!	
3. P—Q4	P—Q4

Double-edged. In allowing the B to be exchanged, White gives the QP solid protection and obtains chances on the KB-file. It works well in this game, but since my game against Donner at the Lugano team tournament 1968 I am not so sure about the value of this move.

| 6. ..., | N—B4 |
| 7. B—Q3 | P x P(?) |

Donner took the B without this inferior exchange. As a result he reserved the option between a later PxP and P—B5 and also denied the white N access to the strong square QB3.

8. P x P	N x B
9. P x N	B—K2
10. O—O	O—O
11. N—B3	B—Q2
12. R—B1	P—B4
13. P x P e.p.	R x P

Obviously based on a miscalculation, this move allows White the strong central push in the centre.

14. P—K4!

When Littleton saw this move made on the board he (a) complained to the tournament director that I had played P—K4 twice in one game and (b) on returning to his own game he upset his cup of coffee over board, opponent and self. I had not realized that the move was so strong!

14. ...,   **N x P**

This was Black's idea. After the game he suggested 14. ..., PxP; 15. NxP, R—R3; but this is obviously bad. The R is quite out of play (a King-side attack being impossible), and the white N on K4 is a tower of strength. Possibly White can even continue with the brutal 16. P—KN4, causing the venturesome R no end of trouble.

| 15. N x N | Q—N3 |
| 16. B—N1 | B—B4 |

Here Black had intended to continue with 16. ..., QR—KB1?; and only now perceived that 17. RxR,

BxR; could be answered with 18. P—K5!, BxP; 19. N—K2, when Black's own B obstructs the KP and he cannot regain the piece.

17. N—K2   **B—N4**

If now 17. ..., P—K4; 18. RxR, PxR; 19. PxP, PxN; 20. Q—Q3, P—B4; 21. N—N3! and the white threats mature earlier.

| 18. R x R | QB x N |
| 19. Q x B | B x N ch? |

But this leaves Black a piece down with nothing to show for it. His best chance was 19. ..., PxR; 20. RxB!, QxR; 21. Q—K3!, when White will have two minor pieces for Rook and pawn, which is far from easy to win.

20. R—B2	R—KB1
21. R—B1	P—KR4
22. P x P	P x P
23. Q—B2	Q—KR3
24. K—R1	

Disdaining the preservation of the QNP (24. P—QN3) as unnecessary — which, of course, it should have been. On the other hand, if White was "planning" to make such a muck of the simple ending, he would have been wiser to be less prodigal with his pawns.

24. ...,	B x R
25. R x B	R x R
26. Q x R	Q—B8 ch
27. Q—N1	Q x P
28. Q—Q1	Q—K4
29. P—N3	P—Q5
30. Q—Q3	K—B2
31. K—N2	K—K2
32. Q—K4	Q x Q ch
33. B x Q	P—QN4
34. K—R3?	

This is typical of the disjointedness that marks the usual "non-master" game. White had enough time on the clock to sleep for an hour in comfort — yet he suddenly develops the *idee fixe* that he needs the K to stop a non-existent contingency of being left with one, or possibly two, unqueenable pawns on the KR-file after total dissolution of material on the Q-side. Simple centralization of the K would have won without difficulty. Thus the fascinating ending that follows is due to bad play rather than careful strategy.

34. ...,	P—N5
35. K—R4	P—QR4
36. B—B2	K—Q3
37. K x P	K—B4
38. K—N6	K—B5
39. K x P	K—B6
40. B—N3	K—N7
41. P—KR4	P—Q6

During the game both of us were under the delusion that the immediate 41. ..., P—R5; 42. BxP, KxP; would lose time after 43. B—N5, but after 43. ..., P—N6; exactly the same ending would have been reached.

42. P—R5	P—R5
43. B x P	K x P
44. P—R6	P—N6
45. B x P ch	K x B
46. P—R7	P—Q7
47. P—R8(Q)	P—Q8(Q)

Thus all White has saved of his tremendous superiority is the pawn on KN3. Both Patterson and myself felt the same thing: "If only I had studied the famous ending Botvinnik-Minev (Amsterdam 1954) a little more closely — but who expects something like this to crop up?" We had no endgame literature available except the perfectly useless Fine who—like everybody else twenty-five years ago — regards the ending of Q+NP vs. Q as a draw because he — like everybody else twenty-five years ago — tries to use the K to protect the pawn and roams the board with the Q; whereas it is the Q that should accomplish the shepherding of the pawn (from a central square) and the K that has to do the roaming. Both of us knew OF the modern analyses in connection with the two Botvinnik games mentioned

above, and some of the principles governing them, but that was as far as our knowledge went.

Meanwhile, with my enormous time advantage, we have not yet reached the adjournment stage, the following somewhat loosely-played moves still being made in the first session:

48. Q—QN8 ch	K—R6
49. Q—R7 ch	K—N7
50. Q—N6 ch	K—R6
51. Q—K3 ch	K—N7

Even these early exchanges make it clear that Patterson does not repeat Minev's mistake of keeping the K on the 4th and 5th ranks (which would make White's task considerably easier), but further back.

52. Q—K5 ch	K—R6
53. K—B6	Q—Q7
54. K—B5	

White does not yet perceive that the check on KR6 is quite harmless — see move 57.

54. ...,	Q—Q6 ch
55. K—B4	

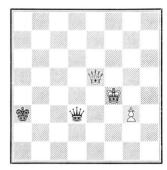

This was the sealed move at last. Patterson had by now run short of time for the second time in this session and was relieved at having at last a chance of looking up his woefully inadequate literature. So indeed was I, though not for long. In fact, I abandoned "the book" after about five minutes and began to study the position instead. The conclusions I reached

102

were that the K of the stronger side could always reach *some* position where the checks came to an end as long as the pawn was fairly far back, where it interfered with certain checks (compare e.g. the position on move 60) — but that this process became progressively more difficult as the pawn advanced. Well, we would have to cross that bridge when we came to it.

55. ...,	Q—B8 ch
56. K—N5	Q—B8 ch
57. K—B6!	Q—R3 ch
58. K—B7	Q—R2 ch
59. K—B8	Q—R3 ch
60. Q—N7	

The first check to the checks: that on Q3 is impossible because the white Q would interpose on the K-Q-diagonal; while on KB4 the P stands guard. Black must therefore make a non-committal move, allowing White to get his Q back to the centre (a very important step in all these operations) and then advance the pawn.

60. ...,	Q—QB3
61. Q—K7 ch	K—N6
62. Q—K3 ch	K—R7
63. Q—K2 ch	K—R6
64. P—N4	Q—R3 ch
65. K—B7	Q—B5 ch
66. K—N6	Q—Q3 ch
67. K—R5	Q—Q4 ch
68. P—N5	

Another square conquered, but Black had no better check. Before advancing the pawn, White made quite sure that the Queen would soon be available to offer her umbrella again: that, in other words, Black could not force a sequence of checks that would compel the white K to guard his pawn permanently. In the circumstances Black renounces a check altogether, preferring to keep the pawn pinned, but this does not help for long.

68. ...,	Q—KB4
69. Q—K3 ch	K—R5?

This is clearly bad; the K should again go back to the 7th rank, as will be clear on move 73. I was surprised that my opponent was resorting to such experiments at this late stage.

70. K—R6!	Q—B1 ch
71. K—N6	Q—N1 ch
72. K—B5	Q—B2 ch
73. K—N4	Q—KN2

After 73. ..., Q—Q2ch; 74. K—N3!, the checks are at an end again, for 74. ..., Q—B2(Q3)ch would be answered with 75. Q—B4ch. This could not have happened if the black K were safely at QR7. Now White gets his P to the 6th rank with the K well behind it, which is very advantageous: in the closing stages of this ending the K has to abandon the pawn altogether and approach his royal colleague with mating designs.

74. Q—K4 ch	K—R6
75. P—N6	

This is as favourable a position as White can obtain: the Q protects the pawn from as centralized a position as possible, and the K is completely free of any entanglements with the pawn which might restrict his freedom of action.

75. ...,	Q—Q2 ch
76. K—N5	Q—Q1 ch
77. K—B5	Q—KB1 ch
78. K—N4	Q—B1 ch

The past few moves show that White is still fumbling, but now he makes up his mind and brings the K across to the other wing.

79. K—N3!	Q—B2 ch
80. K—B3	Q—KN2

Again the checks are at an end, and the blockade of the pawn cannot be maintained.

81. K—K3	K—N6
82. Q—Q3 ch	K—R7
83. K—Q2!	Q—R3 ch
84. K—B2	Q—R7 ch
85. Q—Q2	

This is the device first pointed out

by Botvinnik in his analyses: the white K is brought to the same rank (or diagonal) as the black K so that, on an interposition of the Q, he can then discover check on the next move.

85. ...,	Q—B2 ch
86. K—Q1 dis ch	K—N6
87. Q—Q3 ch	K—N7
88. Q—Q4 ch	K—N8
89. P—N7	

Again the pawn is protected by the Queen.

89. ...,	Q—B8 ch
90. K—K2	Q—B7 ch
91. K—K1	

Here my opponent *resigned*, much to my surprise. Objectively the decision is fully justified, but I am far from sure that I would not have fallen into one of the traps still open in this position:

Clearly Black could not play 91. ..., Q—N6; 92. Q—Q1ch, nor 91. ..., Q—N7; 92. Q—Q1ch, followed by a check on the second rank. There are, however, two more promising ways of trying to stop the pawn from Queening. One is 91. ..., Q—B1; when the winning procedure brings out the Botvinnik stratagem in full flower: 92. Q—N1!, Q—KN1; 93. K—B2 dis ch, K any; 94. Q—N2! (the discovered check motif again!), K any; 95. K—N1! This trick of playing the white K to the first square of the file on which the P is placed — with the Q between K and P — I first saw in Wade's win against Van der Pol, at Enschede 1961, though, as Roycroft points out in the letter quoted, it is much older and does, in fact, go back to Philidor! In this position the blockading Q has no check, while the white Q cannot be stopped from giving a check from the KB-file and then going to KB8.

This leaves the defence 91. ..., Q—N3! Both my opponent and I were quite satisfied that this could be answered by a check on the QR2—KN8 diagonal followed by the Queening of the pawn. It was only when I prepared the game for the British Chess Magazine that I woke up to the fact that on 92. Q—N4ch, K—R8!; 93. Q—R3ch, K—N8; 94. Q—N3ch, K—R8; 95. P—N8(Q), there would follow 95. ..., Q—KN8ch!; 96. K—Q2, Q—B7ch; 97. K—B3, Q—Q5ch!; 98. K—B2, Q—Q7ch!; 99. KxQ stalemate.

This discovery shocked me so much that I expressed my doubts whether this ending might not finally be saved by the stalemate threat, but A. J. Roycroft (as well as several other correspondents, including my opponent) pointed out the winning method on 91. ..., Q—N3: 92. Q—N4ch, K—R8; 93. Q—R5ch!, K—N8; 94. Q—N5 ch, K—R8; 95. Q—K5ch, K—N8; 96. Q—N8ch, K—R8; and now simplest 97. Q—R8ch and 98. P—N8 (Q), though White can be clever and play 97. P—N8(R)! — but not 97. P—N8(Q) because of another stalemate trap: 97. ..., Q—K5ch; 98. K—B2, Q—K6ch; 99. K—N2, Q—R6ch; etc. In other words, White must force the Queening of the pawn not by playing the Queen to QN3 but by checking down to the eighth rank. If, in this line, Black tries 93. ..., K—N7; 94. Q—K5ch, K—B7; there follows 95. Q—B7ch, K—Q6; 96. Q—Q8ch, K—K6!; 97. Q—Q2ch; (but not 97. P—N8(Q)?, Q—QN8ch; 98. Q—Q1, Q—N5ch; 99. K—B1, Q—QB5 ch!!; 100. QxQ — with a stalemate in the middle of the board!), K—B6; 98. Q—B2ch, forcing exchange of Queens on the next move.

Getting involved in this ending and the subsequent correspondence had an amusing aftermath. At the Lugano team tournament 1968 I had a long four-session battle with the Hungarian grandmaster Bilek, which after White's

127th(!) move reached the following position: White (Bilek): K on QN3, Q on Q6, P's on QB3, QB6. Black: K on KR8, Q on KN7. White's position is clearly won (the second pawn not even being required), but less well alerted to the traps inherent in this sort of ending, Bilek answered my 127. ..., Q—N1ch; with 128. P—B4?, and after 128. ..., Q—N6ch! had to allow stalemate.

Game No. 47.

Played at Copenhagen in 1967, in a heat of the Europa Cup (on the first occasion an Irish team participated in this competition), this game was the first (and only one) in which I had to defend my favourite line in the French against a grandmaster. The result shows how difficult it is to break the black build-up. As it happened, the game was the last to finish — it cost the West German team the qualification for the finals in favour of Denmark.

White: W. Unzicker.

French Defence.

1. P—K4	**P—K3**
2. P—Q4	**P—Q4**
3. N—QB3	**N—KB3**
4. B—N5	**B—K2**
5. P—K5	**N—N1**
6. B—K3	**P—QN3**
7. Q—N4	

Unlike Letelier (game No. 43), Unzicker plays the Q to the K side, which leads to quite different motifs.

7. ...,	**P—N3**
8. N—B3	

But he does not follow up with the stereotyped P—KR4, reasoning that Black will have to play P—KR4 himself anyway, when White retains the possibility, P—KR3—KN4.

8. ...,	**B—R3**
9. O—O—O	**B x B**
10. KR x B	**P—KR4**

It is amusing to compare the relative state of the white and black development: White every piece, Black one Bishop! This consideration, however, is quite meaningless as long as White is unable to open the game. Naturally Black must be on guard against any such opening even if it is effected at the cost of material.

11. Q—N3	**Q—Q2**
12. B—N5	**QN—B3**

Just as in game No. 43 Black is in no hurry to play P—QB4 once the white-squared B is off the board. A possibility was 12. ..., P—QB3 (to prevent a sacrifice on Q5); followed by BxB, Q—K2, N—Q2 and O—O—O.

13. Q—B4!

Threatening to open central squares by B—B6. Black must therefore exchange the Bishop which was meant to guard the weakened black squares.

13. ...,	**B x B**
14. N x B	**N—Q1!**

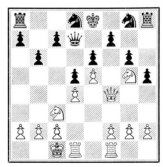

This paradoxical move, which seems to delay O—O—O *ad infinitum*, was one of the hardest to find in my whole chess career. Why not, one is inclined to ask, the simple 14. ..., Q—K2; to be followed by 15. ..., N—R3; and then O—O—O? In that case White's tremendous lead in development could be made to tell by 14. ..., Q—K2?; 15. NxQP!, PxN; 16. P—K6! Then Black cannot give up the Queen for a

105

"bag of wood" by 16. ..., PxP; 17. NxP, QxN; 18. KR—K1, QxR; 19. RxQch, because after 19. ..., K—Q2 (19. ..., KN—K2; 20. Q—B6!, K—Q2; 21. Q—K6ch, is merely a transposition of moves); 20. Q—B7ch, KN—K2; 21. Q—K6ch, K—Q1; 22. P—QB4!, R—K1; 23. PxP, QNxP; 24. Q—K4, he loses another piece. And if he tries 16. ..., P—B3; 17. N—B7!, R—R2; 18. Q—B3! (18. ..., N—Q1; 19. QxQP, P—B3; 20. Q—B3, R—B1; 21. Q—N3), he lands in a terrible mess.

15.	P—KR3	P—QB3
16.	P—KN4	Q—K2
17.	Q—Q2	N—R3
18.	R—R1	N—N2

At last the road is open for the King.

19.	P—B4	O—O—O
20.	Q—K2	P x P
21.	P x P	QR—K1

Threatening to unscramble the position by the thematic P—B3, which White can do nothing to stop.

22.	R—R4	P—B3
23.	P x P	Q x P
24.	Q—K5	Q—K2!

Both Unzicker and I were convinced that after 24. ..., QxQ; 25. BPxQ, the black game would be lost, but the text, which threatens 25. ..., N—B2; was planned when I played 21. ..., QR—K1.

25.	Q—K1	N—B2
26.	R x R	N x R
27.	Q—K5	N—B2
28.	N x N	Q x N
29.	R—R1	K—Q2
30.	N—N1	

So as to control both K4 and QB4 — the absence of the white-squared Bishops makes itself felt.

30.	...,	N—Q3

At last this N — which has merely been in the way of other pieces for most of the game — comes into its own on this powerful post.

31.	N—Q2	R—KB1
32.	P—N3	

Once again the black position looks critical (naturally, if he tries 32. ..., N—K5?; there follows 33. NxN, PxN; 34. R—B1! — while the KBP is immune because of the threat R—R7ch). But there is a simple way out. After the game we thought that 32. P—B3 (to protect the QP in the coming events) might have been better, but after 32. ..., N—B5; 33. NxN, PxN; 34. R—B1, the black game is perfectly playable.

32.	...,	P—B4!

The second thematic pawn push of the French to the rescue! With the cosy square B3 thus available to the black K, White has to protect his KBP and kiss the R-file good-bye.

33.	R—B1	Q—B3
34.	Q x Q	R x Q
35.	P—N5	R—B1
36.	N—B3!	N—B2!
37.	R—R1	

Back to the R-file, in a last attempt.

37.	...,	P x P
38.	R—R7	K—Q3
39.	N—R4	

Or 39. NxP, P—K4! In either case Black is in time to nullify the play of the white pieces.

39.	...,	R—KR1

"Remis?" said Unzicker. "Remis," said I. White will have to play 40. RxN, RxN; for 40. RxR, NxR; 41. K—Q2, P—K4!; 42. P—B5, PxP; 43. P—N6, NxP; 44. NxN, would give only Black chances. The R ending should be drawn with reasonable play, and since Unzicker intended to leave very early next morning there was no point in prolonging the game.

When, in the post-mortem, I mentioned that things might have been easier for me after P—QB3 (as given in the note to Black's 12th), he said: "Why worry? You solved the defensive problem perfectly."

Game No. 48.

Eisinger's pawn sacrifice in the Giuoco Piano is one of the least frequently seen gambit lines — and one of the most promising! It leads to slow positional pressure rather than a violent piece attack and may be neglected for this very reason. For the usual gambiteer wants to have his fun, and the careful positional player is loth to "invest" material. The following game from the Irish Championship, Dublin 1968, is not a true test of the line, since Black's 8th move has been known for many years to be inferior.

Black: Ray Byrne.

Giuoco Piano.

1. P—K4	P—K4
2. N—KB3	N—QB3
3. B—B4	B—B4
4. P—B3	B—N3

This and the following move introduce the "strongpoint defence" in which Black counters all White's efforts to inveigle him into PxQP. Compare the game against Euwe (No. 15).

5. P—Q4	Q—K2
6. P—Q5!?	N—N1
7. P—QR4	

Usually the gambit is played without this move and this is better, because after White plays the QN to R3 he would threaten both N—B4 and N—N5. In the present game square QN5 is already protected and the moves of the respective QRP's help Black to get counter play on the QN-file. That the black KB loses all pawn protection is of less importance.

7. ...,	P—QR3
8. P—Q6!	

The logical follow-up to the 6th move. Unless White blocks the opponent's development with this sacrifice, he should not have opened the diagonal of the black B.

8. ...,	P x P?

Black's game will be so constricted that he should exploit every opportunity to exchange pieces. 8. ..., QxP!; is the accepted move. With the two QRP's still on their original squares, a game Ahues-Van der Bosch, Nauheim 1935, continued 7. ..., QxP; 8. QxQ, PxQ; 9. N—R3, N—KB3; 10.

B—Q5, NxB; 11. PxN, K—K2; but in this line, too, White should first play 9. N—N5!

9. N—N5!

Forcing the black N to unnatural squares and thus safeguarding the blockading position of the B bound to appear on Q5, this move is much stronger than the immediate development of the QN.

9. ...,	N—R3
10. B—Q5	N—B3
11. N—QR3	O—O
12. N—B4	B—B2
13. N—KR3!	Q—B3
14. O—O	R—N1
15. P—B4	

Black has made virtually forced moves all the time and has had no time to disentangle his Q-side. Now White gains further time through the threat of 16. PxP.

15. ...,	Q—R5
16. P—B5	P—QN4
17. P x P!	

Exchanging pawns before making his combination gives the white R an open file, which is of importance in

Position after Black's 17th move.

the note to Black's 27th move.

17. ...,   P x P

See diagram on previous page.

18. B—N5   Q—N5

19. Q—Q2!

A combination introduced by a quiet move and continued with another quiet move.

19. ...,   P x N

20. P—B6!   Q—R4

The only move to hold on to the piece for the time being — but not for long.

21. P x P   K x P

22. B—B6 ch   K—N1

22. ..., K—N3; is worse, e.g. 23. R—B3, B—Q1; 24. BxN!, and the white Queen enters on Q6. Or 23. ..., N—N1; 24. QR—KB1, NxB; 25. RxNch, K—N2; 26. R(1)—B5, Q—R5; 27. P—KN3!, QxN (27. ..., QxR; 28. RxQ, KxR; 29. Q—N5 mate); 28. Q—N5ch, K—R1; 29. RxBP, B—N3 ch; 30. K—R1, and wins.

23. R—B3   B—Q1

24. R—N3 ch   N—N5

25. B x B   N x B

26. Q—K2   K—R1

27. R x N   Q—R3

Here I expected 27. ..., RxP; 28. R—N8ch, RxR; 29. QxQ, R(1)xPch; 30. K—B1, RxP; but the combination is quite incorrect: 31. Q—N5, N—K3 (if 31. ..., RxN; 32. QxNch, K—N2; 33. Q—N5ch, K—B1; 34. K—N1!); 32. Q—B6ch, K—N1; 33. N—B2, P—R4 (if Black gives the R's for Q+N, he loses the B afterwards); 34. R—R8!, R—N8ch; 35. K—K2, R—N7ch; 36. K—Q1, R(either)xN; 37. RxBch, N—B1; 38. BxPch, K—R2; 39. B—N8ch!, and mate in two.

28. R—KB1

Now White simply masses his forces against the KBP.

28. ...,   N—K3

29. Q—B2   B—R3

30. R—N3   N—B4

If 30. ..., P—B3; 31. R—B3, K—N2; 32. Q—R7.

31. N—N5   N—Q6

If now 30. ..., P—B3; simplest is 31. NxP.

32. N x P ch

Not as elegant as 32. QxP, but just as effective.

32. ...,   R x N

33. Q x R   Resigns.

Game No. 49.

Neither the gambiteers of the classic period of chess nor the stodge merchants of the turn of the century were in the mood for openings that involved giving up the Queen for an assortment of wood. Thus the "image" of the Queen became unduly inflated. Modern opening theory has cleared away the adoration of the Queen as though she were a Madonna; and experimental lines such as the King's Indian variation used by Bronstein against Spassky at Amsterdam 1956 came to be investigated. Played in the Irish Championship at Dublin 1968, the following game shows a similar positional sacrifice previously experimented with by Larsen.

White: B. P. Reilly.

Dutch Defence.

1. N—KB3   P—K3

2. P—KN3   P—KB4

3. B—N2   N—KB3

4. P—QB4   B—K2

5. N—QB3   O—O

6. O—O   P—Q3

7. P—Q4   Q—K1

8. R—K1

The currently fashionable line in the Dutch has now been reached.

8. ...,   Q—N3

9. P—K4   N x P

10. N x N   P x N

11. R x P

Now Black cannot capture the R because of 11. . . . , QxR?; 12. N—R4, when 12. . . . , QxN; 13. PxQ, BxP; does not give Black enough. But with his next move he gains square Q5 for the Queen and White can therefore not maintain the offer.

| 11. . . . , | N—B3 |
| 12. R—K1? | |

This move has been virtually refuted by the combination that follows. Much stronger — among other lines such as 12. R—K2 — is 12. Q—K2, with the continuation, 12. . . . , B—B3; 13. B—Q2!, P—K4; 14. PxP, NxP; 15. NxN, BxN; 16. QB—B3, with which John Moles beat me in the Irish Championship 1969. It is then extremely difficult for Black to meet White's combined play on the K-file and the long white diagonal.

| 12. . . . , | N—N5! |
| 13. B—Q2 | |

An interesting novelty; in the students' world championship Rejkjavik 1957 and in the game Nejkirch-Larsen, Portoroz 1958, 13. P—QR3, was played with the same follow-up. Reilly's move gives up another pawn so as to get play for his pieces at the end of the following deal:

13. . . . ,	N—B7
14. N—R4	B x N
15. B—K4	N x KR!
16. B x Q	N—B6 ch
17. K—N2	P x B
18. P x B	N x P ch
19. K—N1	N—B6 ch
20. K—N2	

Here Mednis-Martin at Rejkjavik repeated moves (except that the pawn was on QR3 and the B on QB1 — as also in the Larsen game). Larsen, with his N on KB4 — Nejkirch having played the K to N3 instead of N1 on move 19 — realised the great potential of the black position and played 20. . . . , P—QN3; winning after a long fight in 72 moves. The white pieces never got any real play at all. In the text position I was aware of the fact that in taking the pawn I would allow the white pieces dangerous play which, however, I believed could be contained, after which the important extra pawn would guarantee victory.

20. . . . ,	N x QP!
21. B—R5	P—B4
22. B—B7	N—B4

Safeguarding the QP, since 23. BxP, is punished by 23. . . . , R—Q1.

23. Q—R4	P—K4!
24. R—Q1	R—B3!
25. Q—K8 ch	K—R2
26. R—Q3	

White has developed all his units with strong threats, but these have achieved nothing, and Black is now ready to hit back.

| 26. . . . , | N—Q5 |
| 27. R—K3! | |

To stop Black developing his B with tempo. Thus, if it were Black's move, he could have played 27. . . . , B—B4; 28. QxR, BxR; 29. QxRP, R—B5!; 30. BxP, R—N5ch; 31. K—R3, R—N8; and White is powerless against B—B8ch and N—B4 mate. Black's difficulty is that he cannot develop the B Larsen's way, by P—N3, because of 28. K—B1, when 28. . . . , B—N2; or B—R3; would allow 29. R—R3 mate. The mutual threats on White's KR3 are a feature of the following passages.

| 27. . . . , | N—B6! |

Now Black threatens 28. ..., B—R6ch; or, if White captures twice on his KB3, B—N5ch. If White answers 28. K—R1, N—R5!; with early mating threats, while the white counter-threat on KR3 is gone for good. And if White relinquishes the 8th rank by 28. Q—K7, there would follow 28. ..., B—N5!; 29. BxP, N—R5ch; followed by 31. ..., N—B4. This leaves only the text move.

28. K—N3	N—Q5
29. K—N2	N—B6
30. K—N3	N—Q7!

Decisive — White can only play the hapless King all the time.

31. K—N2	N x BP
32. R—KN3	N—Q7
33. Q—K7	N—K5
34. P—KB3(!)	

34. R—KB3, B—B4!; is obviously hopeless. The text is designed to clean up all Black's centre pawns in return for the exchange, but unfortunately after the great bloodletting the black pieces are all trained on the naked white King.

34. ...,	N x R
35. P x N	B—K3
36. B x P	B—Q4!
37. B x KP	R—B2
38. Q x BP	B x P ch
39. K—R2	R—K1
40. Q—B3	B—B3
Resigns.	

For if — so as to stop the mate threatening with R—B8 and R—KR8 — White plays 41. P—KN4, R—B7ch; 42. K—N1, R—N7ch; 43. K—B1, R—B1ch; 44. K—K1, R—B6; 45. Q—B5, R—KR6; and wins. Or if 41. B—B4, R—K7ch; 42. K—N1, R—Q2; 43. Q—N3, B—N4!; and wins (44. K—B1, RxP dis ch). Or if 41. K—N1, R(2)—K2; 42. B—B4, R—K8ch; and mate next move.

Game No. 50.

Played at the Ballyclare Week-end Tournament 1968, the following game is probably the best purely positional achievement of my whole career and as such makes a fitting conclusion to this little collection. Black chooses a passive opening line and is gradually forced to the wall.

Black: P. Henry.
French Defence.

1. P—K4	P—K3
2. P—Q4	P—Q4
3. N—QB3	P x P
4. N x P	P—QN3

Occupation of the long white diagonal is one of the motifs behind the exchange on Black's 3rd move, but this move is usually deferred for a while.

5. N—KB3	B—N2
6. B—Q3	N—KB3
7. Q—K2	

Contrary to appearances, Black could not answer 7. NxNch, with 7. ..., QxN?; 8. B—N5, for if then 8. ..., BxN; 9. Q—Q2!, wins the black Queen. But the simple and solid-looking 7. ..., PxN; improves Black's hold in the centre as well as giving him the open N-file whereas the doubling of the pawn is of little significance.

7. ...,	QN—Q2
8. B—KN5	B—K2
9. O—O	N x N
10. B x N	

If Black exchanges both Bishops, he cannot then retake on KN5 because his QR remains *en prise.*

10. ...,	B x KB
11. Q x B	O—O
12. B x B	Q x B
13. P—B3	

Here John Moles asked me whether this was to be another contribution to *Grosse Remispartien* (adv.) — appar-

110

ently not realizing that despite the minor piece bloodletting White has preserved a substantial edge. Square K5 is firmly in his grip; an eventual P—QB4 by Black would give White the Queen-side majority, and the only real trump Black usually has in this type of position, control of the long white diagonal, has been drawn.

13. ...,   N—B3

With this move Black renounces any chance of playing P—QB4, with the result that he is gradually crushed. But on 13. . . . , P—QB4; 14. QR—Q1, White would also have excellent chances.

14. Q—B6!   QR—N1

If 14. . . . , Q—Q3; 15. N—K5, maintains the bind. With the text Black tries to chuck out the Queen by getting the KR to the Q-file, but his Rooks land on poor squares in the process.

15. P—QR4	KR—Q1
16. KR—K1	R—Q3
17. Q—B4	P—B3

17. . . . , P—B4; is no longer feasible: 18. PxP, R—B3; 19. P—QN4!, PxP; 20. P—N5, with the threat of N—K5—QB6.

18. N—K5	Q—N2
19. P—QN4	P—QR3

Again 20. P—N5, was an unpleasant threat, but now the black Q-side is fixed in another unenviable position: the white-square weaknesses are transformed into black-square weaknesses.

20. P—R5	P—QN4
21. Q—Q3	Q—K2
22. Q—N3	

Now the threat of 23. NxQBP! enables White to bring the N via Q3 to B5 without losing a tempo with the protection of his QBP against a possible N—Q4.

22. ...,	QR—Q1
23. N—Q3	R—Q4
24. N—B5	R—R1
25. R—K5?	

One move too early! White should first make sure of his back rank by 25. K—B1! (not so good would be 25. P—R3, because it shortens the KR-file on which a white R will have important business later on).

25. ...,   R x R?

Black misses the chance of getting a little relief. He should play 25. . . . , N—Q2!; for if then 26. RxR, KPxR!; 27. Q—B7, R—K1!; protecting the Q and threatening mate on the back rank. If then 28. N—Q3, N—B3!; 29. QxQ (not 29. QxP?, Q—K7!), RxQ; 30. N—B5, R—R2; 31. R—K1, K—B1; the black position is much easier to defend than in the text. If White had played the precautionary K—B1 first, he could answer the move KPxR with R—K1, winning at once. The mutual omissions show to what extent the tactical element enters into the most positional game.

26. Q x R   N—Q4

Now 26. . . . , N—Q2; is unplayable because of 27. Q—B7. In the ensuing part of the game White will get much better value out of his N than Black.

27. Q—N3	Q—B2
28. Q x Q	N x Q
29. K—B1	K—B1
30. K—K2	K—K2
31. K—Q3	N—K1
32. R—K1	N—Q3
33. P—KB4!	

Now the weakness on K3 (as well as that on KR2) will be added to those on the Q-side.

33. ...,	R—R2
34. P—N4	P—N3(?)

After this further weakening of the pawn position the game is demonstrably lost. For better or worse, he had to try 34. ..., K—B3.

35. R—K3

It is now obvious how important the unobstructed R-file will turn out to be.

35. ...,	K—B3
36. R—K5	N—B5
37. P—N5 ch	K—K2

The King has to remain in the centre. I had not clearly decided what to play after 37. ..., K—N2; but had tentatively planned 38. N—K4!, sacrificing the exchange so as to enter the Queen side after 38. ..., NxRch; 39. QPxN, R—Q2ch; 40. N—Q6, followed by K—Q4—B5. Analysis shows this to be unanswerable.

38. R—K2	N—Q3
39. R—K3	K—B1
40. N—K4!	

With the P position irremediably fixed, Black must be stopped from ultimately playing his N to Q4, hitting both BP's. White has squeezed every ounce of advantage out of his minor piece and is now prepared to go over to the R ending.

40. ...,	N x N
41. R x N	K—K2
42. R—K5	K—Q3
43. R—K3	R—R1
44. R—R3	R—R1
45. K—K4	

Zugzwang!

45. ...,	P—R4
46. P x P e.p.	P—B4 ch
47. K—Q3	R—R2

47. ..., K—Q4? ; 48. P—R7 — *Zugzwang.*

48. P—B4	K—Q2
49. P x P	BP x P
50. P—Q5	

This was my sealed move. The ending still becomes interesting, though at first glance it looks quite lost for Black.

50. ...,	P x P
51. K—Q4	K—Q3
52. R—R4	

And again *Zugzwang*. Black chooses the only line that makes a fight of it.

52. ...,	K—K3!
53. K—B5	K—B3
54. R—R3!	

The fruit of some hard adjournment analysis, this move has a threefold purpose: it temporarily keeps the white K in touch with the QP and thus in some variations allows White to get into a P ending with the remote passed P; it stops the R being *en prise* when the NP advances, and it gives the R, cut off on R4, a wide sweep along the third rank. I think it is the only move to win.

54. ...,	P—N4
55. P x P ch	K x P
56. R—N3 ch	

So that if now 56. ..., KxP; 57. R—R3ch, K any; 58. RxR, KxR; 59. KxP, and wins the P ending; while 56. ..., K—B5; would lose to 57. R—N6!

56. ...,	K—B3
57. K—N6	P—B5
58. R—QR3	K—K4
59. K x P	K—K5
60. K x P	P—B6
61. P—R6	P—B7
62. R—R1	P—Q5
63. K—R5	K—K6
64. P—N5	K—K7
65. P—N6	P—B8(Q)
66. R x Q	K x R
67. P—R7	P—Q6
68. P—R8(Q)	P—Q7
69. Q—B3 ch	K—K8
70. Q—K3 ch	**Resigns**

White does not have to play the Q ending after 70. Q—K4ch, and 71. QxR (now or later), for if 70. ..., K—Q8; 71. K—N4!, K—B7; 72. Q—N3ch, K—B8; 73. K—B3 and wins.

LIST OF OPPONENTS
(Numbers Refer to Pages.)

LIST OF OPENINGS

(Numbers Refer to Pages.)